Society at a Glance 2009

OECD SOCIAL INDICATORS

ORGANISATION FOR ECONOMIC CO-OPERATION AND DEVELOPMENT

The OECD is a unique forum where the governments of 30 democracies work together to address the economic, social and environmental challenges of globalisation. The OECD is also at the forefront of efforts to understand and to help governments respond to new developments and concerns, such as corporate governance, the information economy and the challenges of an ageing population. The Organisation provides a setting where governments can compare policy experiences, seek answers to common problems, identify good practice and work to co-ordinate domestic and international policies.

The OECD member countries are: Australia, Austria, Belgium, Canada, the Czech Republic, Denmark, Finland, France, Germany, Greece, Hungary, Iceland, Ireland, Italy, Japan, Korea, Luxembourg, Mexico, the Netherlands, New Zealand, Norway, Poland, Portugal, the Slovak Republic, Spain, Sweden, Switzerland, Turkey, the United Kingdom and the United States. The Commission of the European Communities takes part in the work of the OECD.

OECD Publishing disseminates widely the results of the Organisation's statistics gathering and research on economic, social and environmental issues, as well as the conventions, guidelines and standards agreed by its members.

> *This work is published on the responsibility of the Secretary-General of the OECD. The opinions expressed and arguments employed herein do not necessarily reflect the official views of the Organisation or of the governments of its member countries.*

Also available in French under the title:
Panorama de la société 2009
LES INDICATEURS SOCIAUX DE L'OCDE

Foreword

*T*his is the fifth edition of Society at a Glance, the biennial OECD compendium of social indicators. This report attempts to satisfy the growing demand for quantitative evidence on social well-being and its trends. It updates some of the indicators included in the 2001, 2003, 2005 and 2006 editions. It adds some new ones, including indicators of height, perceived health status, risky youth behaviour and bullying. In addition, a new set of headline social indicators are developed, providing an overview of social well-being and its trends. This report also includes a guide to help readers in understanding the structure of OECD social indicators, and a special chapter on leisure time across the OECD. More detailed information on all indicators, including those not in this edition, can be found on the OECD web pages (www.oecd.org/els/social/indicators/SAG).

This report was prepared by Simon Chapple and Maxime Ladaique. As this report addresses a wide range of topics, it would have been impossible to complete without the contributions of many people in and outside the OECD Social Policy Division. These include Francesca Colombo, Michael De Looper, Marco Mira d'Ercole, Justina Fischer, Michael Förster, Pauline Fron, Rie Fujisawa, David Jonathan Gonzalez-Villascan, Ingrid Herrbach, Maria del Carmen Huerta, Herwig Immervoll, Gaetan Lafortune, Pascal Marianna, Marlène Mohier, Dominique Paturot, Dominic Richardson, and Olivier Thévenon. Mark Pearson, Head of the OECD Social Policy Division, originally developed and has subsequently supervised the reports.

This book has...

StatLinks

A service that delivers Excel® files from the printed page!

Look for the *StatLinks* at the bottom right-hand corner of the tables or graphs in this book.
To download the matching Excel® spreadsheet, just type the link into your Internet browser,
starting with the *http://dx.doi.org* prefix.
If you're reading the PDF e-book edition, and your PC is connected to the Internet, simply
click on the link. You'll find *StatLinks* appearing in more OECD books.

Table of Contents

Country codes

AUS	Australia
AUT	Austria
BEL	Belgium
CAN	Canada
CZE	Czech Republic
DNK	Denmark
FIN	Finland
FRA	France
DEU	Germany
GRC	Greece
HUN	Hungary
ISL	Iceland
IRL	Ireland
ITA	Italy
JPN	Japan
KOR	Korea
LUX	Luxembourg
MEX	Mexico
NLD	Netherlands
NZL	New Zealand
NOR	Norway
POL	Poland
PRT	Portugal
SVK	Slovak Republic
ESP	Spain
SWE	Sweden
CHE	Switzerland
TUR	Turkey
GBR	United Kingdom
USA	United States

ISBN 978-92-64-04938-3
Society at a Glance 2009
OECD Social Indicators
© OECD 2009

Chapter 1

Headline Social Indicators

Introduction

In the 1970s and 1980s, social indicators were developed to provide a better tool than conventional market income indicators for the assessment of living and working conditions. Today the various issues of *Society at a Glance* provide rich information on social conditions in different OECD countries and on the measures taken to improve them. This richness, however, comes at a price. It is difficult for readers to get a concise picture of how social conditions compare across countries and evolve over time from a quick scan of *Society at a Glance*.

A sub-set of headline indicators gives a more parsimonious representation of social conditions. This sub-set serves an important communication function, rapidly alerting users to some of the critical challenges in the social field confronting various OECD countries, and highlighting comparative progress.[1]

This chapter presents the headline indicators as an integral part of *Society at a Glance*. It then describes the approach used to select and construct the set of headline social indicators.

Headline social indicators across the OECD

Tables 1.1 and 1.2 present the eight selected headline indicators, two for each of the four organising dimensions used in *Society at a Glance*. These tables allow readers a bird-eye scan of social conditions across countries, both at a point in time (Table 1.1) and in terms of changes over time (Table 1.2).

In Table 1.1 "Traffic lights" characterise the most recent performance at a point in time of each OECD country (Table 1.1). "Green circle" lights are used for countries that are in the top three deciles of performance, "red diamond" lights for those that are in the bottom three, and "yellow triangle" lights for those in the middle four deciles.

In Table 1.2 "Arrows" describe changes in performance over a recent period compared with other OECD countries. "Green arrows pointing up" characterise countries in the top three deciles of performance, "red arrows pointing down" refer to those in the bottom three deciles of performance, and "yellow arrows pointing to the right" highlight those countries whose change in performance put them in the middle four deciles.

As the information provided is qualitative, indicator values are not shown.[2] As contextual indicators, the tables also include (on the right) net national income (NNI) in United States dollars (USD) at purchasing power parity (PPP) rates (Table 1.1) and growth in real GDP per capita (as real NNI growth is only available for 17 countries) (Table 1.2).

Table 1.1 shows a variety of patterns. Most countries display *levels* of performance spanning the full range of results (green, yellow and red). Only Australia, Austria, Finland, France, Germany, Norway and Sweden do not record any "red lights". Germany, Mexico, Turkey, the United Kingdom and the United States do not record any "green lights". No country has all green lights, but Denmark, New Zealand and Norway have the highest number, five.

Table 1.1. **Headline social indicators for the most recent period**

These symbols describe countries performance at a point in time, with "green circle" denoting countries in the top three deciles, "red diamond" those in the bottom three, and "yellow triangle" those in the middle four

	Self-sufficiency		Equity		Health		Social cohesion		Income
	Employment to population ratio, total	Share of students with insufficient reading competences	Gini coefficient of income inequality	Gender wage gap	Life expectancy at age 65, men	Infant mortality	Subjective well-being	Crime victimisation	NNI per capita, at USD PPPs
	Levels 2007	Levels 2006	Levels 2004-05	Levels 2006	Levels 2006	Levels 2006	Levels 2006	Levels 2005	Levels 2006
Australia	●	●	▲	▲	●	▲	●	▲	▲
Austria	▲	▲	●	▲	▲	●	▲	●	▲
Belgium	◆	▲	▲	●	▲	▲	●	▲	▲
Canada	●	●	▲	▲	●	◆	●	▲	●
Czech Republic	▲	◆	●	▲	◆	●	▲	..	◆
Denmark	●	●	●	●	◆	▲	●	◆	●
Finland	▲	●	●	▲	▲	●	●	▲	▲
France	▲	▲	▲	●	●	▲	▲	●	▲
Germany	▲	▲	▲	▲	▲	▲	▲	▲	▲
Greece	◆	◆	▲	▲	▲	▲	◆	●	▲
Hungary	◆	▲	▲	●	◆	◆	◆	●	◆
Iceland	●	▲	▲	▲	●	●	▲	◆	▲
Ireland	▲	●	◆	▲	▲	▲	◆	◆	●
Italy	◆	◆	◆	▲	▲	▲	◆	●	▲
Japan	▲	▲	▲	◆	●	●	▲	●	▲
Korea	▲	●	▲	◆	◆	◆	◆	..	◆
Luxembourg	◆	◆	●	●	▲	▲	●	▲	●
Mexico	◆	◆	◆	..	▲	◆	▲	◆	◆
Netherlands	●	●	●	▲	◆	▲	●	◆	●
New Zealand	●	●	◆	●	●	◆	●	◆	◆
Norway	●	▲	▲	●	●	●	●	▲	●
Poland	◆	▲	◆	●	◆	◆	◆	▲	◆
Portugal	▲	◆	◆	▲	◆	●	◆	●	◆
Slovak Republic	◆	◆	●	◆	◆	◆	◆	..	◆
Spain	▲	◆	▲	▲	●	▲	▲	●	▲
Sweden	●	●	●	▲	▲	●	▲	▲	●
Switzerland	●	▲	●	▲	●	▲	●	◆	●
Turkey	◆	◆	◆	..	◆	◆	◆	..	◆
United Kingdom	▲	▲	◆	▲	▲	▲	▲	◆	▲
United States	▲	▲	◆	▲	▲	◆	▲	▲	●

NNI: Net national income.

StatLink ⌦ http://dx.doi.org/10.1787/550750484867

There are also different patterns between countries when looking at changes in these indicators of social conditions. As shown in Table 1.2, most countries span the full range of changes across fields, with Denmark, Finland, Ireland, and Greece recording no red arrows; Austria, Canada, the Czech Republic, and Iceland recording no green arrows; and Poland, Slovakia and Turkey recording no yellow ones. Poland has six green arrows, making strong progress on all headline fronts where there is Polish data.

Table 1.2. **Relative progress in headline social indicators for the most recent period**

Arrows describe changes in performance over time, with " green arrows pointing up" denoting countries in the top three deciles of performance, "red arrows pointing down" denoting those in the bottom three deciles of performance, and "yellow arrows pointing to the right" those in the middle four deciles of performance.

	Self-sufficiency		Equity		Health		Social cohesion		Income
	Employment to population ratio, total	Share of students with insufficient reading competences	Gini coefficient of income inequality	Gender wage gap	Life expectancy at age 65, men	Infant mortality	Subjective well-being	Crime victimisation	Real GDP per capita
	Change 2007/2003	Change 2006/2003	Change 2004-05/2000	Change 2006/ early 2000s	Change 2006/2000	Change 2006/2000	Change 2006/2000	Change 2005/2000	Change 2006/2000
Australia	⬆	➡	⬆	⬇	⬆	⬇	➡	⬆	➡
Austria	➡	➡	..	➡	➡	➡	⬇	➡	➡
Belgium	➡	➡	..	..	⬆	➡	⬆	⬇	⬇
Canada	➡	➡	⬇	➡	➡	⬇	⬇	➡	➡
Czech Republic	➡	⬇	⬇	➡	➡	➡	➡	..	⬆
Denmark	➡	⬆	➡	➡	➡	➡	➡	➡	➡
Finland	⬆	⬆	➡	➡	⬆	➡	⬆	⬆	➡
France	⬇	⬇	➡	⬇	⬆	➡	➡	⬆	⬇
Germany	⬆	⬆	⬇	⬇	⬆	➡	⬆	➡	⬇
Greece	⬆	➡	⬆	..	➡	⬆	➡	..	⬆
Hungary	⬇	➡	➡	⬆	⬇	⬆	⬇	..	⬆
Iceland	➡	➡	..	..	⬇	➡	..	..	⬆
Ireland	⬆	➡	..	⬆	⬆	⬆	➡	..	⬆
Italy	➡	⬇	⬇	..	⬇	⬇	⬆	➡	⬇
Japan	➡	⬆	..	⬇	➡	⬇	⬇	⬆	⬇
Korea	⬇	⬆	..	➡	⬆	➡	➡	..	⬆
Luxembourg	⬇	➡	➡	..	⬆	⬆	⬆	⬇	➡
Mexico	➡	⬆	⬆	..	⬇	⬆	⬇	⬇	⬇
Netherlands	➡	⬇	⬆	⬆	⬆	➡	⬆	⬇	⬇
New Zealand	⬆	➡	➡	⬇	➡	➡	..	➡	⬇
Norway	➡	⬇	⬇	..	⬆	⬇	⬇	⬇	➡
Poland	⬆	⬆	..	⬆	⬇	⬆	⬆	⬆	⬆
Portugal	⬇	⬇	..	..	➡	⬆	⬇	➡	⬇
Slovak Republic	⬆	⬇	..	..	⬇	⬆	⬆	..	⬆
Spain	⬆	⬇	..	..	➡	➡	➡	⬆	➡
Sweden	➡	➡	⬆	⬇	⬇	⬇	➡	⬆	➡
Switzerland	⬇	⬆	..	➡	⬆	⬇	⬇	⬇	⬇
Turkey	⬇	⬆	..	..	⬇	➡	⬆	..	⬆
United Kingdom	⬇	⬇	⬆	⬆	➡	⬇	➡	➡	➡
United States	⬇	➡	⬇	⬆	⬇	⬇	⬇	⬇	➡

Note: The time periods for examination of changes differ somewhat because of data availability. Changes refer to arithmetic differences except for crime victimisation (average annual changes). Some criminal victimisation country data starts earlier than 2000. See the discussion for CO3 in Chapter 8 below. These facts mean that comparability is less than for the levels data.

StatLink ⟨⟩ http://dx.doi.org/10.1787/550810385458

Eight headline indicators

Concisely summarising social conditions through a set of headline indicators is a challenge. In all cases, the goals are: *i)* to describe *outcomes*; *ii)* to inform about the *broad* set of measures included in the four dimensions of the OECD social indicators taxonomy (self-sufficiency, equity, health and social cohesion); *iii)* to cover the *largest possible number* of OECD countries; and *iv)* to allow monitoring of how social status *evolves over time*.

The *selection* of indicators may be based on a statistical analysis. For example, one approach might involve looking at the correlations between all outcome indicators covered in *Society at a Glance*, selecting those characterised by the highest correlation with other indicators within each domain. An alternative approach could rely on some type of factor analysis to indentify suitable combinations of elementary indicators within each domain.

Once selected, decisions are needed as how best to *present* these indicators. Indicators could be "normalised" so that they all conform to a 0-1 scale. Such normalisation also readily permits creation of composite indices for each of the four domains of social indicators, or an aggregate one across the four domains.[3] Normalisation, however, causes a loss in terms of transparency and hence hampers communication.

Meeting the goals described above is also constrained by data availability. First, changes in definition and sources mean that fewer of the indicators of *Society at a Glance* are available in a consistent form over time. Second, many of these indicators are not updated frequently or even at predictable intervals and have limited country coverage. Last, many of these indicators focus on very specific outcomes (*e.g.* suicides) whose effect is already partly captured by others (*e.g.* life expectancy).

Because of these constraints, rather than using statistical criteria the selection of headline indicators is based on a cross-country consensus arising out of a member country consultation process. To meet their communication function, the selected indicators are presented in their raw form, without any normalisation. However qualitative markers are used to ease interpretation of their numerical values. To achieve the desired parsimony, indicators were limited in number for each dimension.

Based on the above considerations, two headline indicators were selected for each of the four dimensions of social indicators (self-sufficiency, equity, health and social cohesion). This makes a total of eight headline indicators to compare social conditions across countries and to assess how conditions have been evolving. The qualitative considerations that have guided the headline indicator selection are described below.

Self-sufficiency

People's self-sufficiency mainly depends on access to jobs and on their skills. With respect to work, a suitable indicator of labour market outcomes is the **employment rate for the working-age population**. This indicator, based on comparable labour force survey definitions, is available yearly for all OECD countries. Relative to other measures of labour market slack like unemployment rates, the employment rate is less affected by people's decisions to withdraw from the labour market when job prospects are poor.

The most comprehensive measure of peoples' skills and competences currently available is the average years of schooling of working-age people. This indicator, however, ignores human capital formation provided outside schools, and neglects schooling quality.[4] Further, to the extent that the skills of people of working age affect their labour market outcomes, these skills are partially captured by employment rates. There are good reasons for focusing on the competencies of people *before* they enter the labour market. Pre-employment competencies provide an indication of future labour market prospects and life opportunities. Measures of these competencies for 15-year-olds are available through the OECD *Programme for International Student Assessment* (PISA). These measures are based on comparable survey modules fielded every three years and cover all OECD countries. The indicator used is the **share of students aged 15 with reading competencies at levels 1 or below**, i.e. below the minimal level needed to perform normal activities in daily life. Compared to other (PISA) measures of students' competences, this indicator has the advantage of focusing on those youths who, upon reaching adulthood, are more likely to be unemployed, in low-paid jobs, or dependent on social assistance.

Equity

Equity is a concept relevant to a broad range of outcomes, such as income, health, and education. But few of the equity measures currently available have broad country coverage, good comparability, and are available at regular intervals. The two indicators selected focus on income inequality and on pay differences between men and women.

Differences in income between people living in each country are an obvious manifestation of differences in living conditions. When these differences become too large, they may conflict with shared notions of equity. Data on the distribution of household disposable income is collected by the OECD quinquennially. The data enable comparison of income inequality in all OECD countries and an assessment of changes (since 2000) for around two-thirds of them. The indicator is the **Gini coefficient of household disposable income**. This indicator provides a good summary of the entire distribution of household income, and is well correlated to relative poverty measures. However, the Gini coefficient and its changes are not *perfectly* correlated with other measures of inequality, such as poverty, at a country level (for example, Norway is an outlier in a correlation of changes in the Gini against changes in poverty). Thus choice of the Gini over these other measures of inequality can impact on country rankings in the headline indicators. Additionally Gini coefficients are not intuitively understood.

Indicators of income inequality are based on the assumption that all members of the same household share the available resources. Hence, by construction, these measures are not suited to assess differences among men and women, which are an important dimension of equity in all OECD countries. To describe these gender differences, the indicator reported is the **ratio of median earnings between women and men working full-time**. While this is only one element of the labour market penalty confronted by women, it can be more easily compared across countries, and is available at regular intervals. On the other hand, it misses equalisation on account of men and women sharing incomes within families. Data on gender wage gaps are available through the *OECD Earnings Database* for 19 OECD countries.

Health status

The two main dimensions of health status are mortality and morbidity. Unfortunately, no comprehensive, regularly available measure of morbidity currently exists.[5] For this reason, the two indicators used focus on mortality risks for people at the two extremes of the age spectrum.

With respect to older people, the indicator is **life expectancy at age 65**, which is available through *OECD Health Data*. Minor drawbacks of this indicator are that no series currently covers the entire elderly population and that for a few countries the series is not annually updated.[6] With respect to children, the indicator is the **infant mortality rate**, i.e. the number of deaths of children under 1 year of age, expressed per 1 000 live births. One potential problem with infant mortality rates is due to differences across countries in the way deaths of premature babies are registered, although the importance of this issue for data comparability may be exaggerated (see the discussion for indicator HE3.1 in Chapter 7 below).

Social cohesion

Social cohesion has both positive and negative dimensions. On the positive side, it includes people's participation into community life and their attitudes to others. On the negative side, lack of social cohesion may be revealed by a variety of pathologies such as suicides, risky behaviours or crime.

No comprehensive measure exists of people's participation in community life or of their attitudes to others. Research has however documented that several of these features – together with personal attributes – contribute to the life satisfaction of people. For this reason, the indicator measuring positive dimensions of social cohesion is **average life satisfaction** in different countries. Levels of life satisfaction are based on country scores in the 2006 *Gallup World Poll*. Data for measuring changes in life satisfaction comes from a variety of sources (see Box 1.1). While this indicator is, admittedly, only an indirect measure of people's participation in community life and of their attitudes to others, the other indicators available have less intuitive appeal.

Box 1.1. **Measuring life-satisfaction changes**

Time series data on life satisfaction were not available from the 2006 *Gallup World Poll*, used to examine life-satisfaction levels in *Society at a Glance* 2009. Hence data on changes in life satisfaction was constructed from other sources. The initial source was a variety of data collated by the World Database of Happiness (WDH) (see *www1.eur.nl/fsw/happiness/ hap_nat/nat_fp.htm*). Data was extracted from the WDH site on 3rd and 4th October 2008.

Changes in life satisfaction were examined over the period from 2000-06. It was thought that this was a sufficiently lengthy period for changes in satisfaction to emerge. An additional reason was that the chosen end period, 2006, also coincides with the Gallup Survey.

Data on changes in life satisfaction were available for 28 OECD countries. The WDH had 20 countries' time series data taken from the *Eurobarometer* survey. All but Turkey were European countries. Data for the United Kingdom were for Great Britain only. Another four countries had data originally from the *World Values Survey* (Canada, Korea, Mexico and the United States). Norwegian and Swiss data was from the *European Social Survey*. Australian data was from the *Australian Unity Wellbeing Index* and Japanese data was from the *Life in Nation* survey. Data were not available for Iceland and New Zealand.

The original *Eurobarometer* life-satisfaction scale was 1-4, as was the Japanese data, and the transformations provided by the WDH to a 0-10 scale were used. The original *World Values Survey* had a 1-10 scale, and again the same WDH transformation to a 0-10 scale was used. The Australian and Norwegian data needed no transformation.

The questions, translated into in English, differed marginally across surveys. The *Eurobarometer* asked: "How satisfied are you with the life you lead?", while the *World Values Survey* asked "All things considered, how satisfied are you with your life-as-a-whole right now". The Australian survey asked "All things considered, how satisfied or dissatisfied are you with your life as-a-whole these days". The Canadian, Swiss and Norwegian surveys asked the WVS question, and the Japanese survey asked the *Eurobarometer* question.

Box 1.1. **Measuring life-satisfaction changes** (cont.)

Out of necessity, change data for the Czech Republic, Hungary, Poland, the Slovak Republic and Turkey was for the period 2001-06. Mexican data was also for a five-yearly period – 2000-05. Japanese data was for the years 2001-07. Korean data was for a four yearly period 2001-05, Norwegian data for 2002-06, and Swiss data was for 200/03-2006/07. United States data was for 1999-2006. For the remainder of the countries, 17 in total, data was for the desired period, 2000-06.

Seasonality was a further limitation. The *Eurobarometer* data were mostly reported in the WDH as being collected in April or April-May 2000 and in Spring 2006, which roughly equate seasonally. The *Eurobarometer* data for the four countries where data was for the period 2001-06 were for October 2001 and Spring 2006. The Australian data compared September 2000 to October 2006. The Canadian data were for August 2000 and an unknown period during 2006. The Japanese data compared September 2000 to July 2006. The Swiss data were collected between September 2002 and February 2003 and August 2006 and April 2007. Korea data for 2001 were for November. No information was provided as to the collection period for the 2005 Korean data. Norwegian data were collected for September 2002 and August to December 2006.

Despite these differences, it was judged that the additional country observations were worth the reduction in average data quality from the various compromises mentioned above. However, the data issues need to be borne in mind by readers, and the detailed country ranking data on life-satisfaction changes should be considered with the appropriate caution.

The correlation between the end point life-satisfaction data used to calculate changes (mostly 2006, but also 2005 and 2007) was fairly strongly correlated with the Gallup Poll data ($r=0.81$). Major outliers included Turkey and Mexico.

The highest change reported in the data is the very large *Eurobarometer* rise in Turkish life satisfaction from 4.6 in 2000 to 6.1 in 2006. A second Turkish survey (via the *World Values Survey*), using a 1-10 life-satisfaction scale, showed a parallel, even larger rise from 5.6 in 2000 to 7.5 in 2007. The *Eurobarometer* 2006 survey ranks Turkey above Greece, Hungary, Portugal and Slovakia On the other hand, *Gallup World Poll* data show Turkey in 2006 with the lowest level of life satisfaction in the OECD.

Almost all the surveys used here involved small samples sizes (in the handful of thousands). It is not clear which of the reported changes in life satisfaction are statistically significant.

The headline indicator measuring the negative manifestations of social cohesion is crime victimisation, *i.e.* the **share of people who have been victims of a criminal offence** in the preceding calendar year. The data are drawn from the *International Crime Victim Survey* which in its most recent wave covers 26 OECD countries. The indicator used here refers to the ten crime categories that are covered in all waves of the survey.

Notes

1. Headline indicators are used in other areas of OECD work. For example, the OECD report *Environment at a Glance – OECD Environmental Indicators* includes a narrow set of (10) "key environmental indicators", endorsed by OECD Ministers as a tool for public information and communication.

2. Readers interested in numerical values of the headline indicators are referred to the relevant chapters on the detailed indicators below and on the OECD web pages (*www.oecd.org/els/social/indicators*).

3. An example of a "composite" index based on 16 OECD social indicators is presented in Chapter 2 of *Society at a Glance* 2006.

4. Measuring these competencies would require surveys covering the entire population and available for most OECD countries. The OECD *Adult Literacy and Life Skill Survey* (ALLS), run in 2003, covered only five OECD countries. The OECD *Programme for the InternationalAssessment of Adult Competences* (PIAAC) will allow an indicator of competences for the entire adult population in the future.

5. One possible measure of morbidity is provided by self-reported health. While information on this variable is available through *OECD Health Data*, these data do not allow sufficiently regular comparisons over time.

6. For this reason, the indicator presented in Table 1 below refers to elderly men *only*. Obvious alternatives would be to present an indicator of life expectancy in old age for women, or deriving a measure that combines the experience of both men and women.

ISBN 978-92-64-04938-3
Society at a Glance 2009
OECD Social Indicators
© OECD 2009

Chapter 2

Special Focus: Measuring Leisure in OECD Countries

The amount and quality of leisure time is important for people's well-being for the direct satisfaction it brings. Additionally, leisure, taken in certain ways, is important for physical and mental health. Leisure also contributes to the well-being of people other than the person directly enjoying leisure. When a person engages in leisure, the benefits gained are shared with others in a multitude of ways, including improvements in personal relationships, family functioning, and in terms of creation of social capital networks (at least from some types of shared leisure). Leisure time patterns across the OECD therefore warrant investigation as an important part of social monitoring.

What exactly then is leisure? Leisure may be defined in terms of time, activities, or states of mind. In terms of time, leisure can be seen as time spent free of obligation and necessity. For example, the quantity of leisure has been defined as "all activities that we cannot pay somebody else to do for us and we do not really have to do at all if we do not wish to" (Burda et al., 2006, p. 1). Despite its advantages, this definition does not specifically mention the types of activities that can qualify as leisure. Nor does it describe the extent to which a person is free from obligation. Alternatively, leisure can be defined as specific activities conventionally thought of as "leisurely". A more thorough definition may be based on what the majority of people would list as leisure activities, such as television watching, participating in sports or exercise, reading, seeing movies, and so on. Finally, leisure can be defined as a state of mind, meaning engaging in enjoyable or pleasurable activities. The actual measures of leisure used here draw on all these definitions.

This chapter first provides a short literature review of the economic determinants of leisure time. It then examines leisure across the OECD as the residual time not spent in paid work. This residual approach to the data is not ideal, in particular because it does not allow cross-country or inter-temporal variations in amounts of unpaid work undertaken. However, the residual approach does allow considerations of leisure for the largest possible cross-section/time series of countries across the OECD. A further contextualisation of leisure time is then undertaken, considering a very broad-brush allocation of time over the adult life cycle. This contextualisation is done for an average OECD country in terms of years before compulsory education, years of schooling, years before labour market entry, years not in paid work, years in work, and years in retirement for males and females.

For the smaller subset of 18 OECD countries for which comparable data could be obtained, time-use studies are used to more accurately explore leisure during a typical day and across time (the annex to this chapter provides some comparative details of the 18 time-use surveys used). These time-use surveys precisely measure the time devoted to both market and non-market activities by recording data on people's time allocation when in or away from their jobs. Respondents' descriptions of activities are coded into sets of general categories such as "time spent in work", "time spent doing household chores", or "time spent in leisure activities". While methodologies and approaches vary to a certain degree, all the time-use surveys used in this chapter define the "leisure" category as the sum of non-compulsory activities such as hobbies, watching television or listening to the radio, socialising with friends and family, attending cultural events, hosting events, and practising a sporting activity. All the surveys aim to closely measure what people actually do with their time, not what they recollect having done with it long after the events. Once adjusted, this data makes it possible to compare cross-national leisure levels and trends. Still employing time-use data, the second part of this chapter focuses on patterns of leisure distribution by categories of both gender and age.[1] This part of the chapter also details the types of leisure activities people engage in and the satisfaction they derive from accomplishing them. Finally some consideration is made of the relationships between leisure and other measures of well-being, and leisure and policy choices about paid holidays.

The economic theory of leisure time

Since Veblen's *Theory of the Leisure Class* at the end of the 19th century, economists and other social scientists have taken a great deal of interest in leisure. Most work on labour supply in the neoclassical tradition focuses theoretical and empirical attention on the labour/leisure choice. However, this approach traditionally ignores other uses of time. It effectively examines the margin between paid work and all other uses of time in aggregate ("residual time"), which of course include leisure time as a sub-set, in terms of the constrained optimisation techniques of neoclassical economics (see Caussa, 2008 for recent OECD work in this vein).

The canonical modern treatment of time-use, explicitly addressing leisure in a more sophisticated fashion, can be attributed to Gronau (1976). Drawing on the earlier work of Mincer, Gronau argues for a need to distinguish between unpaid work (home production) and leisure. He suggests that the justification for focusing only the paid work/residual time choice, a focus with which he disagrees, is based on an assumed stability of the allocation of residual time between competing uses (such as home production, leisure, and sleep) in response to economic changes. Gronau develops a formal model with a three-fold distinction between leisure, home production, and paid work. His model is based on the assumption that marketed goods obtained from paid work and home produced goods are perfect substitutes. An increase in market wages reduces home production. The wage impact on both leisure and market work is indeterminate. An income rise increases leisure, reduces paid work, and leaves home production unchanged. Empirical work by Bloch and Gronau using United States and Israeli data suggests that leisure amongst couples is positively related to the husband's wage income, negatively related to the wife's wage income, and positively related to non-wage income. In addition, higher numbers of children, and especially pre-school children, reduce leisure time (Gronau, 1976, Table 1).

Other extensions of labour supply models to incorporate home production include Chiappori (1997) and Apps and Rees (1996, 1997, and 2002). In addition to market work, home production, and leisure time, Gronau's model has also been extended to cover work-related travel time by Solberg and Wong (1992). Their empirical results do not concur with their model predictions, and the authors suggest that this is mainly due to the violation of their assumption (shared with Gronau) of perfect substitutability between market work and home production.

None of the models presented above include sleep in their consideration of leisure. As Biddle and Hamermesh (1990) point out, many labour supply models assume a fixed amount of time is allocated between paid work and waking leisure. By implication, sleep is a fixed biological constant, yet theory and evidence do not support this. Biddle and Hamermesh theoretically and empirically show that sleep time, as with other forms of time usage, responds to marginal economic incentives. If this is the case, some sleep also becomes a leisure-like activity. As such, several very recent time-use studies have categorised *all* sleep as leisure (see Aguiar and Hurst, 2007; Engler and Staubli, 2008).

Trends in residual of paid work time

The analysis commences by considering maximum leisure time as simply the amount of time that is not spent in paid work. While some immediate limitations of this approach are obvious – it fails to consider unpaid work for example, as well as time spent commuting – its advantage is that data on hours worked are available on a comparable basis for a large number of OECD countries for long time periods. Good comparisons both across countries and across time are possible. From this initial definition of leisure as the residual time-not-worked it is possible to progressively build a more solid conceptual approach which in turn allows a study of leisure levels and trends which is, however, less broad in terms of OECD country coverage.

It is possible to estimate total annual hours of paid work for full-time equivalent workers across a large number of OECD countries and thus calculate the associated residual (see Table 2.1). Of course, an evident limitation of this approach is that it says nothing about leisure, even as a residual value, for large and varying parts of the population of each country that are not actually in employment. There are numerous features of interest in Table 2.1. First there are considerable differences in annual hours of work of all the employed across the countries. The standard deviation of the residual leisure measure across the countries considered is 175 hours or about four weeks of work at forty hours of work a week. The lowest residual leisure is found in the United States, while the highest is in Norway. Other countries with a low amount of residual leisure include Hungary, Poland, and the Slovak Republic. The highest amounts of residual leisure are found in the Nordic countries and western continental Europe: the Netherlands, Denmark, Sweden, and France.

If leisure is considered as nothing more than the time spent away from paid work, then naturally any change in the amount of annual hours worked will be reflected in variations of the amount of available leisure time. Table 2.2 considers average growth rates in hours worked across the OECD from 1970 until 2005. The five-yearly averages chosen remove much of the possible higher frequency business cycle fluctuations. Clearly the data are incomplete, especially for the early period for many countries (1970-85). But the overall pattern shows a declining number of hours worked at a diminishing rate over time for most countries. There are very few countries which have had periods of rising growth in hours of paid work per person. The notion of a general, OECD-wide "time crunch" arising from changing conditions in the paid workforce does not appear to be supported, although a growing time crunch could certainly exist for particular groups.

Figure 2.1 uses the same data to illustrate long-term trends over approximately 30 years in annual hours worked for six selected OECD countries. Canada and the United States follow very similar patterns with comparatively stable hours per person from 1980 onwards. Patterns in the United Kingdom are also quite similar to those in North America.

Table 2.1. **Anatomy of a typical work year for dependent employees, 2006**

Decomposition of average annual hours actually worked by full-year equivalent workers into its components

	Annual hours of work[1]	Annual residual leisure	Average weekly hours on all jobs	Usual weekly hours of work in the main job	Extra hours on main job = Overtime + variable hours (eg. flexible hours) + others	Hours on additional jobs	Annual weeks worked	Holidays and vacation weeks	Full-week absences due to non holiday reasons	Part-week absences due to non holiday reasons	Absences due to sickness and maternity[2]
	(a) = (c)*(g)	(b) = (365*24)-(a)	(c) = (d)+(e)+(f)	(d)	(e)	(f)	(g) = 52 - [(h) + (i) + (j) + (k)]	(h)	(i)	(j)	(k)
	Hours		Weekly hours worked				Weeks worked/not worked				
Australia (2005)	1 733	7 027	36.4	..	..	..	47.6	..	..	..	..
Austria	1 590	7 170	38.8	37.5	0.7	0.5	41.1	7.4	1.7	0.7	1.2
Belgium	1 461	7 299	36.0	35.4	0.3	0.4	40.5	7.1	2.2	0.4	1.8
Canada (2005)	1 579	7 181	36.3	35.6	..	0.7	43.5	3.8	2.2	1.0	1.5
Czech republic	1 754	7 006	41.3	40.4	0.7	0.2	42.5	6.3	1.6	0.2	1.5
Denmark	1 367	7 393	36.2	34.6	0.9	0.7	37.8	7.4	3.4	1.1	2.4
Finland	1 517	7 243	38.6	36.9	1.2	0.4	39.4	7.1	2.4	1.6	1.5
France	1 459	7 301	37.3	36.4	0.6	0.3	39.1	7.0	2.2	1.7	2.0
Germany	1 478	7 282	36.1	34.3	1.4	0.3	41.0	7.5	1.7	0.6	1.1
Greece	1 783	6 977	40.0	39.6	0.1	0.3	44.5	6.7	0.3	0.2	0.3
Hungary	1 889	6 872	41.3	40.6	0.3	0.4	42.6	6.2	1.5	0.2	1.4
Iceland (2006)	1 748	7 012	43.9	41.3	1.2	1.4	39.9	6.2	2.4	1.6	2.0
Ireland	1 543	7 217	35.8	35.0	0.5	0.3	43.2	5.7	1.6	0.3	1.3
Italy	1 536	7 224	37.3	36.8	0.3	0.2	41.2	7.9	1.4	0.3	1.2
Luxembourg	1 541	7 219	37.7	36.7	0.8	0.2	41.0	7.4	1.6	0.5	1.6
Netherlands	1 325	7 435	31.6	29.5	1.6	0.5	41.9	5.3	2.2	0.9	1.6
Norway	1 290	7 470	35.7	33.1	1.9	0.7	36.1	6.5	4.4	1.7	3.3
Poland	1 806	6 954	41.5	40.0	0.4	1.1	43.5	6.2	1.3	0.1	1.0
Portugal	1 675	7 085	40.0	39.0	0.2	0.7	41.9	7.3	1.5	0.2	1.1
Slovak Republic	1 775	6 985	40.8	40.3	0.3	0.2	43.5	6.9	0.7	0.1	0.7
Spain	1 601	7 159	39.1	38.2	0.6	0.3	41.0	6.8	1.9	0.5	1.8
Sweden	1 386	7 374	37.5	35.6	1.3	0.6	36.9	6.8	3.3	1.8	3.2
Switzerland	1 618	7 142	37.8	34.3	2.9	0.6	42.9	6.0	1.4	0.9	0.9
United Kingdom	1 530	7 230	37.5	36.6	0.6	0.3	40.8	6.5	2.1	1.3	1.2
United States[3] (2005)	1 896	6 864	41.3	38.5	2.7	..	45.9	3.8	1.6	..	0.7
OECD25	**1 595**	**7 165**	**38.2**	**36.9**	**0.9**	**0.5**	**41.6**	**6.5**	**1.9**	**0.8**	**1.5**
Coefficient of variation	0.11	0.02	0.07	0.08	0.81	0.62	0.06	0.16	0.44	0.75	0.47

1. See Annex 2.A1 of *OECD Employment Outlook 2004* for a succinct explanation of the method used by the OECD Secretariat to estimate annual actual hours worked per person in employment for Belgium, Ireland, Luxembourg, the Netherlands and Portugal. The same method is applied to estimate annual working hours per employee for all European countries shown in this table.
2. These weeks are already included in columns h and i, but are included a second time in order to correct for an assumed 50% under-reporting (see Annex 2.A1), except for Australia.
3. The estimates refer to total full-time employment. Total week absences due to non-holiday reasons are reported rather than full-week absences.
Source: Secretariat estimates for European countries based on European Labour Force Surveys results and EIRO (2005). Estimates for Australia, Canada, United States based on ECO/CPE/WP1(2007)11/ANN2.

StatLink ᕫᓟᔍᒲ http://dx.doi.org/10.1787/551047830221

Hours worked in Japan by employed people have been falling steeply, converging to United States, Canadian, and United Kingdom levels. French and Norwegian data show no levelling off during the 1980s and the 1990s, but some stabilisation after the millennium.

Table 2.2. **Average annual growth in hours worked per full-time equivalent employee for five-year periods**

	1970-75	1975-80	1980-85	1985-90	1990-95	1995-2000	2000-05
Australia	−0.2	−0.2	−0.1	−0.1	0.0	0.0	−0.7
Austria	..	..	..	..	..	−0.2	0.3
Belgium	..	..	..	−0.5	−0.9	−1.5	0.1
Canada	−0.6	−0.7	−0.1	0.0	−0.1	−0.1	−0.3
Czech Republic	..	..	..	..	..	0.3	−0.9
Denmark	−2.4	−0.3	−0.5	−1.1	−0.2	0.7	0.3
Finland	−0.9	−0.5	−0.4	−0.5	0.1	−0.3	−0.4
France	−1.0	−0.7	−1.2	−0.3	−0.6	−0.7	−0.4
Germany	..	..	..	..	..	−0.8	−0.5
Greece	..	..	..	−0.4	0.1	0.0	−0.3
Hungary	..	..	..	−0.4	0.6	0.2	−0.7
Iceland	−1.5	−1.5	−0.1	−0.2	−0.1	0.6	−1.0
Ireland	..	..	..	0.2	−1.2	−1.7	−0.8
Italy	−1.3	−0.6	−0.6	0.1	−0.5	0.0	−0.5
Japan	−1.2	0.1	−0.3	−0.6	−1.5	−0.7	−0.5
Korea	..	..	0.1	−1.5	−0.2	−1.1	−1.4
Luxembourg	..	..	..	0.0	−0.5	−0.7	−1.1
Mexico	..	..	..	..	..	0.3	0.2
Netherlands	..	..	..	..	−1.6	−0.3	0.0
New Zealand	..	..	..	..	0.3	−0.1	−0.2
Norway	−1.2	−1.8	−0.5	−0.5	−0.2	−0.4	−0.5
Poland	..	..	..	..	..	..	0.1
Portugal	..	..	..	..	−0.7	−1.4	−0.1
Slovak Republic	..	..	..	..	..	−0.7	−0.8
Spain	..	..	−1.5	−0.3	−0.1	0.0	−0.5
Sweden	−1.6	−1.1	0.3	0.3	0.8	0.0	−0.5
Switzerland	−1.0	−0.8	−0.8	−0.4	0.0	−0.2	−0.3
Turkey	..	..	..	..	..	..	..
United Kingdom	−0.6	−1.2	−0.1	0.1	−0.3	−0.4	−0.4
United States	−0.7	−0.3	0.2	−0.1	0.1	−0.1	−0.4
OECD	**−1.1**	**−0.7**	**−0.4**	**−0.3**	**−0.3**	**−0.3**	**−0.4**

.. Not available.

Source: Secretariat estimates based on *OECD Employment Outlook 2006.*

StatLink ᴍᴤ🝿 http://dx.doi.org/10.1787/551055031276

Figure 2.1. **1970-2006: long-term decline in annual hours worked**

Annual hours worked by the total employed population in selected OECD countries

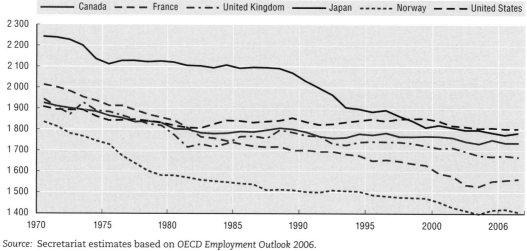

Source: Secretariat estimates based on *OECD Employment Outlook 2006.*

StatLink ᴍᴤ🝿 http://dx.doi.org/10.1787/548525556001

SOCIETY AT A GLANCE 2009: OECD SOCIAL INDICATORS – ISBN 978-92-64-04938-3 – © OECD 2009

Allocation of time over the life course

A second contextualisation for consideration of patterns of leisure from time-use surveys is a consideration of the number of years that people with different characteristics devote to their "main activity" across different life phases. While based on cross-sectional data, the contextualisation can however shed some light on life-cycle patterns of time-use under the very strong assumption that the pattern of experience in terms of labour market outcomes and fertility of a person of a given age (*e.g.* 15) over a particular age range of his or her future life course (*e.g.* 15-64) can be proxied by today's behaviour of the population in that age range (15-64). The underlying assumption is the same as that underlying the calculation of life expectancy or total fertility rates.

Key results are shown in Figure 2.2, which shows how a person's life course can be disaggregated into years spent in different main activities. These data, shown separately for men and women based on averages from those OECD countries for which sufficient data are available, highlight several well-established patterns. Perhaps the best known pattern illustrated is the continuous decline in the number of years in paid work for men and its concomitant rise for women. The rising period in retirement as a consequence of rising life expectancy is shown. Women's earlier retirement age and their longer period in retirement, due both to earlier retirement age and longer life expectancy, are also shown. The likely rise in levels for women's time in education is not shown here. Further work is intended to isolate female educational catch-up in this area.

Figure 2.2. **Years spent in different activities by men and women in a typical OECD country**

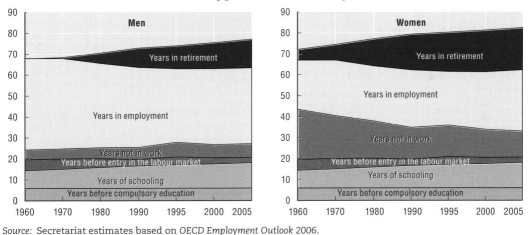

Source: Secretariat estimates based on *OECD Employment Outlook 2006*.

StatLink 📊📉 *http://dx.doi.org/10.1787/548526737374*

Leisure across the average day

The above analysis shows considerable differences in average amounts of paid work across OECD countries over a year. Furthermore, the average annual time spent working has typically declined over the last 30 years. But does a general decline in annual working hours necessarily mean a symmetrical upsurge of available leisure time? The answer is no. The weaknesses of the residual approach in terms of coverage of the population and in assuming that all residual time is spent on leisure are evident. Ultimately this breakdown only offers a partial insight into the elements that have gradually shaped a typical year. Assessing a tangible estimate of the time people specifically allocate to leisure requires the data that only time-use surveys can provide.

In order to better comprehend the share of time dedicated to leisure in a person's average day over an average year, it is important to first see how adults divide their 24 hours among other main activities. The approach taken here is to divide time during the day into five main categories. These five-time categories are 1) Leisure, narrowly defined, 2) Paid work, 3) Unpaid work, 4) Personal care, and 5) Other time (uses of time which are either unaccounted for or undefined). Insofar as complete methodological standardisation and comparability can be attained in time-use surveys, noteworthy cross-national differences *can* be observed in the way people divide their time during an average day. It must be kept in mind that, to varying degrees, time-use surveys' results cannot be regarded as completely accurate in terms of measuring time allocation trends during periods of sickness and/or holidays. Up to date time-use surveys with sufficient information for this study are also only available for 60% of OECD countries (the 18 countries analysed in this chapter) and their methodologies are quite varied. Unfortunately, insufficient information was available to include existing time-use surveys from Hungary, Iceland, and the Netherlands.

"Paid work" includes full-time and part-time jobs, breaks in the workplace, commuting to the workplace, time spent looking for work, time spent in school, commuting to and from school, and time spent in paid work at home. "Unpaid work" includes all household work (chores, cooking, cleaning, caring for children and other family and non-family members, volunteering, shopping, etc.). "Personal care" includes sleep, eating and drinking, and other household, medical, and personal services (hygiene, grooming, visits to the doctor, hairdresser etc.). "Leisure" includes hobbies, games, television viewing, computer use, recreational gardening, sports, socialising with friends and family, attending events, and so on. "Other time" includes all activities not elsewhere mentioned

Figure 2.3 shows that across all 18 OECD countries people spend most time in personal care activities. Variation in the share of time spent in personal care across these countries is comparatively small at 6 percentage points, ranging from a low of 43% of total time in Canada, Sweden, Mexico and Norway to a high of 49% in France.

Figure 2.3. **Share of time taken by leisure and other activities across an average day**

24-hour breakdown of time spent in main activities for all respondents aged 15 and over in 18 OECD countries

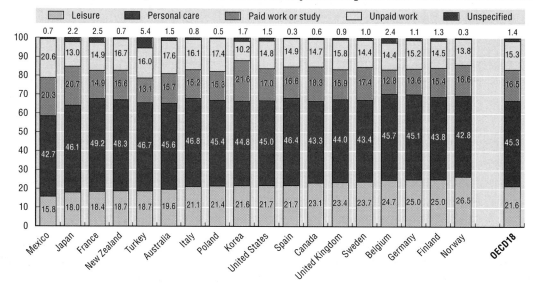

Source: Secretariat estimates based on national and multinational time-use surveys (2006 where available).

StatLink ⚄ http://dx.doi.org/10.1787/548528164155

What activities mainly make up personal care? The primary component of personal care across all countries is in fact sleep. Across the OECD, people sleep an average of 8 hours and 22 minutes per day. Sleep thus accounts for about 77% of average cross-OECD personal care time. The second major component is eating, which accounts for a further 14% of personal care time or 1 hour 37 minutes per day on average across the OECD (Turkey is excluded from this and the following calculations since eating time cannot be separated from other personal care time). Thus sleeping and eating on average make up over 90% of personal care time. The remainder of personal care time covers "Personal, medical and household services". This last category covers various activities such as personal hygiene, going to the doctor, getting a haircut, getting the car repaired, and so on. As some sleeping, eating and drinking, and personal hygiene time could alternatively be classified as leisure (for example, respectively sleeping in, having a long lunch with friends or family, or having one's hair shampooed and cut), there is a considerable element of arbitrariness in the division between personal care and leisure.

Following personal care, leisure is typically the next largest time category, being 22% of time on average across the OECD18. Leisure is highest in Norway at 27% of time and lowest in Mexico at 16% of time. Amounts of leisure are also high in Belgium, Germany, and Finland. At the other end of the spectrum, leisure is also comparatively low in Japan, France, and New Zealand.

Japan and Mexico are the only two countries where paid work represents a higher share of time than leisure, while paid work and leisure represent equal shares in Korea. All 15 other countries report more leisure time than paid work time. On average across the OECD18, paid work time follows in importance after leisure, but the margin is fine. In many countries, for example Mexico, New Zealand, Australia, Italy, Poland, Belgium, and Germany, unpaid work actually absorbs more time than paid work. Mexico is the only country where unpaid work takes up more time than leisure as well.

Of the four largest time categories (leisure, personal care, paid work, and unpaid work), the share of leisure time varies the most between countries, with 11 percentage points difference between Mexico and Norway. The variation in unpaid work time is as great, with an 11 percentage point difference between Korea (low) and Mexico (high). The spread in paid work is smaller, being 9 percentage points between Belgium (low) and Korea (high).

Given the arbitrariness of the personal care-leisure boundary already discussed above, an alternative way of measuring time spent in leisure is to fix personal care at the lowest country rate (42.7% of an average day in Mexico). This lowest country rate of personal care, it could be argued, gives the minimum that might be considered necessary. What is described as a "broad" definition of leisure can then be calculated as the "narrow" leisure already measured and reported above in Figure 2.3 plus the addition of "excess" personal care time over the lowest country rate. The results of this "broad leisure" calculation are reported in Figure 2.4. Average leisure time for the OECD18 rises from 21.6% of time ("narrow" leisure) to 24% of time ("broad" leisure). The range still runs across 11 percentage points from a low of 16% of an average day in Mexico spent in leisure to a high of 27% of an average day in Belgium, but there is more homogeneity of leisure for other countries inside that range.

Some countries gain more leisure time using the broad definition than others. Consequently there are also some considerable changes in country rankings. The biggest upward movers in rankings are France (up nine places), Italy (up six places), and New Zealand (up five places). These three countries move from below average to around or above

Figure 2.4. **A broader definition of leisure raises leisure time and changes country rankings**

Percentage of leisure time in an average day

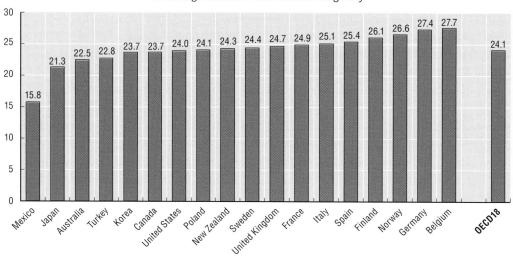

Note: "Broader leisure" refers to daily levels of personal care normalised to the lowest country level. All excess personal care time is re-allocated to the initial leisure value.

Source: Secretariat estimates based on national and multinational time-use surveys (2006 where available).

StatLink 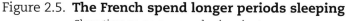 http://dx.doi.org/10.1787/548604870643

the OECD leisure average. The biggest downward moves in terms of broader leisure time include Canada (down six places), and Sweden and Korea (both down four places). In the case of France, the immediate reason for the large change is the very high share of personal care time – the highest in the OECD at 49% of time – some of which is reallocated to leisure. In terms of composition of this high personal care time, of interest are the high amounts of nightly sleep indulged in by the French (which, as noted above, is classified as personal care). The cross-OECD sleep data are shown in Figure 2.5. The average French person sleeps for over an hour a day longer than the Koreans, who sleep the least in the OECD.

Figure 2.5. **The French spend longer periods sleeping**

Sleep time on an average day in minutes

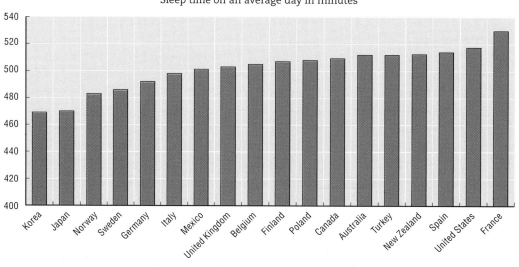

Source: Secretariat estimates based on national and multinational time-use surveys (2006 where available).

StatLink 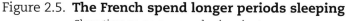 http://dx.doi.org/10.1787/548614043010

SOCIETY AT A GLANCE 2009: OECD SOCIAL INDICATORS – ISBN 978-92-64-04938-3 – © OECD 2009

Another important personal care activity which has already been remarked upon as having leisure-like characteristics in many cultures is eating. Figure 2.6 shows that the range of time spent eating varies by nearly an hour and a half per day between the highest and lowest country. The big upward movers in the broad leisure rankings, France and New Zealand, also both spend a lot of time eating. Each day, the French spend nearly double the time eating than do people in Mexico, Canada, and the United States.

Figure 2.6. **The French spend the most time eating and drinking**

Eating time on an average day in minutes

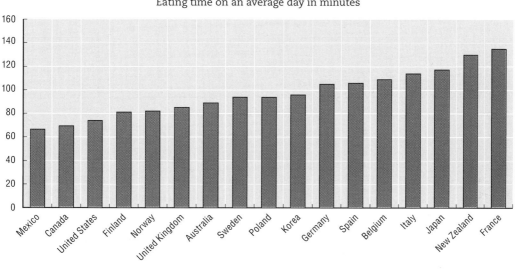

Note: The available time use survey data for Turkey does not separate personal, medical and household care from eating and drinking. The Turkish figure is thus excluded. An *ad hoc* separation out of eating and drinking time based on OECD average shares would give a Turkish figure at around Italian levels.

Source: Secretariat estimates based on national and multinational time-use surveys (2006 where available).

StatLink ᴹᔕᴾ *http://dx.doi.org/10.1787/548621131285*

The last and smallest category of personal care is "Personal, medical and household services". Time spent on such activities ranges, again considerably, from 43 minutes per day in Finland to 77 minutes per day in Korea (see Figure 2.7).

Time trends in leisure from time-use surveys

Another interesting question is the patterns of changes in leisure over time for all adults (a narrow measure is used). This question can be addressed for those few countries that have been conducting time-use surveys over a sufficiently long period of time. These countries are Canada, the Netherlands, Norway, the United Kingdom, and the United States.[2] For each country, long term data are available for periods of different maximum length and frequency. In all cases, the frequency is low, so inferences on longitudinal time trends need to be cautiously drawn. Figure 2.8 indicates that over the past 40 years, the aforementioned countries have experienced different evolutions in terms of shares of time allocated to leisure. The share of time spent in leisure seems to have declined in the Netherlands between the mid-1970s and the early part of the 21st century, with a similar but less pronounced pattern of decline in leisure in the United Kingdom. In Norway leisure is broadly unchanged throughout the period for which data are available. Finally, in Canada and the United States, where data are available over the longest time periods, rising amounts of time are spent on leisure, albeit from a much lower base than the European

Figure 2.7. **Japan and Korea spend more time in personal, medical and household services**

Time spent in personal, medical and household services on an average day in minutes

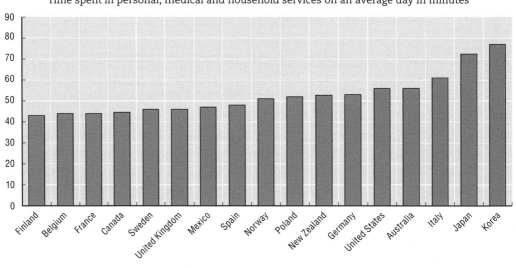

Source: Secretariat estimates based on national and multinational time-use surveys (2006 where available).

StatLink http://dx.doi.org/10.1787/548662533470

Figure 2.8. **Time trends in leisure from time-use surveys**

Long-term trends in shares of leisure in an average day for five selected OECD countries, in percentage

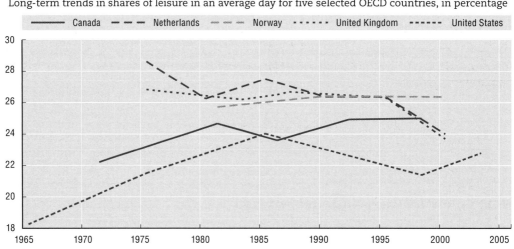

Source: Secretariat estimates based on national and multinational time-use surveys (2006 where available).

StatLink http://dx.doi.org/10.1787/548718113783

OECD countries. Unfortunately, the data are not of sufficient number and frequency to consider leisure in the business cycle context, allowing light to be cast on voluntary and involuntary changes in leisure time

Patterns of leisure distribution

Demographic characteristics and leisure

How does time spent in leisure activities differ across different social groups? This section considers patterns of leisure for different social groups divided by gender and age.

Gender

How does the amount of leisure time differ between men and women across the OECD? There has been a considerable amount of comparative focus on gender differences in paid, unpaid, and total work. But there has been much less focus on gender differences in leisure. Burda *et al.* (2007) use time-use data for Belgium, Denmark, France, Finland, Germany, Italy, the Netherlands, Norway, Sweden, the United Kingdom, and the United States to conclude that "for most rich economies, […] gender differences in the amounts of leisure consumed are tiny" (p. 23). Whether the differences between men and women reported in Burda *et al.*'s study are tiny is a moot point. They report gender gaps in terms of minutes of an average day, chosen to be representative for a year. On a daily basis, the difference in minutes does usually seem small. Annualised, however, it is a different story. The lowest gender gap amounts to 55 annual hours more leisure for men in Norway. It is unlikely that most full time paid workers would consider the equivalent of more than one additional week off work per year as "tiny". Annualising the daily gender leisure gaps – all in favour of men – reported by Burda *et al.* (Tables 1.1 and 1.2) give figures of 116 hours per year in the Netherlands, 128 hours in the United States, 134 hours in Sweden, 170 hours in the United Kingdom, 176 hours in Germany, 195 hours in Denmark, 213 hours in Belgium, 225 hours in Finland, 280 hours in France, and 444 hours in Italy.

Using time-use surveys for 18 OECD countries shown in Figure 2.9 below, men universally report spending more time on activities narrowly classified as leisure than women, an observation consistent with Burda *et al.*'s results. The gender differences here are statistically trivial in Norway (a few minutes a day). By contrast Italian women have nearly 80 daily minutes less leisure time than men. Burda *et al.* (2007, pp. 4-5) have already noted the high amounts of unpaid work of Italian women, and the high levels of time spent watching television for Italian men. As such, much of the additional work of Italian women is apparently spent cleaning the house.

Figure 2.9. **Men have more leisure than women**

Gender differences in leisure time, minutes per day, positive figures show a male advantage

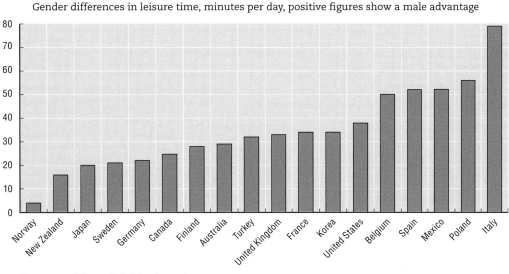

Note: The narrow leisure definition is used.

Source: Secretariat estimates based on national and multinational time-use surveys (2006 where available).

StatLink ⏵ *http://dx.doi.org/10.1787/548724153767*

However, these gender differences in leisure time are also subject to variations according to the way time is categorised as either "Leisure" or "Personal care". So how does personal care differ by gender? Figure 2.10 shows that in a majority of OECD countries, women spend more minutes per day on personal care than men, in some cases – such as Sweden, Belgium and the United States – substantially so. The countries where men spend more time than women on personal care are Italy, Poland, Korea, and Mexico. At nearly half an hour per day, the excess amount of male personal care is especially large in the case of Mexico. Most of the Mexican difference is accounted for by men sleeping 25 minutes more per day than women (Mexicans – men and women combined – sleep at a little below the OECD average per day).

Figure 2.10. **Men generally have less personal care time than women**

Gender differences in personal care time, minutes per day, positive figures show a male advantage

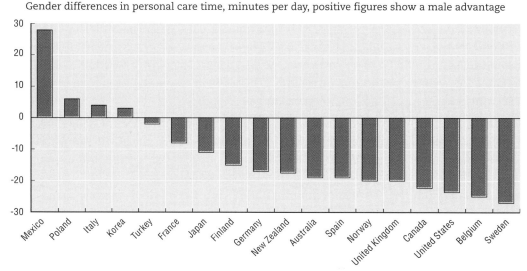

Source: Secretariat estimates based on national and multinational time-use surveys (2006 where available).

StatLink ⌁ http://dx.doi.org/10.1787/548733815678

To examine gender differences in a broader definition of leisure, daily amounts of personal care are again normalised to the lowest country (602 minutes for Mexican women). The excess of any male and female personal care time over this amount is then re-allocated to leisure. This readjustment yields a broader and arguably better measurement of leisure differences between men and women (Figure 2.11).

Despite this adjustment for leisure-like personal care, in the majority of countries examined men still spend more time in broad leisure activities than women. The difference is particularly strong for both Italy and Mexico. Now, however, there are three countries where women have more broad leisure time than men – New Zealand, Norway, and Sweden. The female advantage is only of practical importance in the case of Norway, where on average women have 16 minutes more daily leisure than men. The leisure gender gap in favour of men however remains very large in several countries, notably in Italy, Mexico, Poland, and Korea, and important in many others. It is noteworthy that Italy, Mexico, Poland, and Korea are countries where the pre-existing gender gap in narrowly-defined leisure time increases with the inclusion of the gender gap for personal care. Thus, regardless of whether one uses a broad or narrow definition of leisure, in most countries men tend to have more leisure than women.[3]

SOCIETY AT A GLANCE 2009: OECD SOCIAL INDICATORS – ISBN 978-92-64-04938-3 – © OECD 2009

A remaining limitation in considering gender differences in leisure time arises from the possible gendered nature of shopping as a leisure activity. In the above analysis, all shopping is allocated to unpaid work. It thus reduces leisure, all other things being equal. It is also known from time-use surveys that women shop more than men. For example, in the United States men shop for 43 minutes per day, while women shop for 59 minutes per day. The respective figures for Germany are 49 minutes for men and 66 minutes for women, for Italy 33 minutes for men and 53 minutes for women and for the Netherlands 36 minutes for men and 53 minutes for women (Burda et al., 2007, Table 1.1).[4] It is possible that some of this shopping time has a leisure component and this shopping-as-leisure is generally larger for women.

Figure 2.11. **Men generally have more broadly-defined leisure than women**

Gender differences in broadly-defined leisure time, minutes per day, positive figures show a male advantage

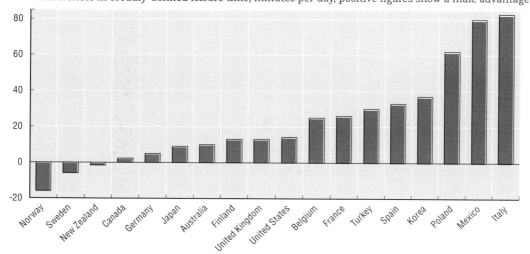

Note: "Broadly-defined leisure" refers to daily and gender-specific levels of personal care normalised to the lowest country level and all excess personal care time is re-allocated to the initial leisure value for both genders.

Source: Secretariat estimates based on national and multinational time-use surveys (2006 where available).

StatLink 📊 http://dx.doi.org/10.1787/548741477728

Leisure patterns by age

To obtain a true picture of leisure over the life time, longitudinal data comprising the entire human life cycle would be warranted. However, such data are not available. In their absence, cross-sectional time-use data by age cohorts can give some indication of how leisure might vary during the different parts of a person's life cycle. Not surprisingly, the young and especially the elderly spend more time on leisure than people of working age. Across all 18 OECD countries analysed in Table 2.3, people aged 65 and over on average consistently spend more time on leisure than all other age categories. Percentages of time spent in leisure peak at 39% in Canada, Norway and Poland. At 25% of total time, those over age 65 have the lowest leisure in Mexico.

The share of leisure time for the 15 to 24-year-old population is generally higher than for working-age cohorts. Predictably, leisure time for young people is always higher than for 25 to 44-year-olds. Perhaps more surprisingly, discrepancies are considerably less important compared to those aged 45 to 64, even though most or all of this older age group is not yet at the official retirement age. The greater absence of young children in the

Table 2.3. **The young and the elderly have more broad leisure time than the working-age population**

Shares of leisure time of people by age, percentage shares of total time in a day

	15-24	25-44	45-64	65 and over
Australia	27	17	22	34
Belgium	28	23	29	38
Canada	27	18	23	39
Finland	30	23	27	38
France	27	22	25	37
Germany	29	23	29	37
Italy	30	21	25	37
Japan	21	16	19	34
Korea	24	22	25	33
Mexico	18	11	16	25
New Zealand	30	20	22	35
Norway	29	24	28	39
Poland	28	22	26	39
Spain	28	20	26	35
Sweden	29	21	25	38
Turkey	. .	. .	. .	. .
United Kingdom	27	22	26	36
United States	27	20	23	37
OECD18	**27**	**20**	**25**	**36**

Note: The table uses broad leisure levels obtained by using Norway's level of personal care as a minimum level and allocating any excess personal care above this to leisure.

Source: Secretariat estimates based on national and multinational time-use surveys (2006 where available).

StatLink ᵃˢ⁹ http://dx.doi.org/10.1787/551073760502

families of the older working-age group is likely to be a strong factor behind the higher leisure time they enjoy relative to the younger working-age group. Finland, Italy and New Zealand stand out with high shares of leisure for young people, with 30% or more of an average day spent in leisure activities. The lowest share of leisure time for young people is found in Mexico, 9 percentage points below the OECD18 average.

Those aged 25 to 44 have more leisure time in countries where it could be argued that specific public policy arrangements have pushed for a more balanced approach to one's professional life or, alternatively, where marginal tax rates are very high: Norway (24%), Finland, Belgium, and Germany (all three at 23%) lead in this age category (Parnanen et al., 2005).

Types of leisure activities

What are the popular leisure activities? Are there big differences in the leisure activities people undertake across OECD countries? Table 2.4 groups time spent in leisure by five major leisure categories: multimedia entertainment at home (TV or radio at home), other leisure activities (various hobbies, internet use, phone conversations, etc.), visiting and/or entertaining friends (both in private and public venues), participating in and/or attending social events (such as concerts, cinema, museums, etc.), and sports (actively participating in regular physical activities, whether individual or organised).

On average across the OECD18 watching TV or listening to the radio is marginally the most popular leisure activity at nearly 40% of time. Watching TV absorbs a high of 48% of time in Mexico and goes as low as 25% in New Zealand.

Table 2.4. **Watching television is the preferred leisure activity across all surveyed OECD countries**

Prevalence of different types of leisure activities percentage shares of total leisure time

	TV or radio at home	Other leisure activities	Visiting or entertaining friends	Participating / attending events	Sports
Australia	41	47	3	2	6
Belgium	36	42	8	8	5
Canada	34	34	21	2	8
Finland	37	40	7	8	8
France	34	45	6	7	8
Germany	28	46	4	15	7
Italy	28	48	6	10	8
Japan	47	42	4	0	6
Korea	35	41	16	1	7
Mexico	48	33	10	4	5
New Zealand	25	45	24	2	5
Norway	31	33	14	15	8
Poland	41	38	6	8	6
Spain	31	41	4	12	12
Sweden	31	42	7	11	8
Turkey	40	25	34	0	2
United Kingdom	41	39	7	10	4
United States	44	32	16	2	5
OECD18	**36**	**40**	**11**	**6**	**7**

Source: Secretariat estimates based on national and multinational time-use surveys (2006 where available). It is important to point out that conclusions derived from these figures should be tentative: national time-use surveys' methodologies differ in the way they choose to include or exclude the measure of secondary activities.

StatLink 🖘📉 *http://dx.doi.org/10.1787/551081652177*

"Other leisure activities" are on average also very popular. This popularity is in part due to the fact that this is a catch-all category which includes hobbies, computer games, recreational internet use, telephone conversations, arts and crafts, walking pets, and so on. Other activities take up to 48% of people's leisure time in Italy, but only 25% in Turkey. Given its size as a category, it would have been of a great deal of interest to present the other category by major sub-categories. Unfortunately this sub-categorisation was not possible due to insufficient consistency across countries in terms of definitions of major sub-categories.

Visiting and entertaining friends, which reaches a high of 34% in Turkey and a low of 3% in Australia, is extremely variable between countries.[5] More "active" types of leisure such as attending cultural events and participating in sports are much less prevalent in all surveyed OECD countries. Attending or hosting cultural events is relatively frequent in Germany and Norway while the practice is much rarer in Japan, Korea and Turkey. The same could be said of sports, which take up 12% of people's leisure time in Spain and only 5% in Belgium, Mexico, New Zealand and the United States.

Satisfaction with time spent on different activities

While the various activities mentioned above provide rich insights into the way people choose to spend their time, no conclusion can be directly reached concerning the satisfaction derived from engaging in various activities (*i.e.* the "state of mind" approach to leisure mentioned in the chapter's introduction). Assessing the relationship between well-being and allocation of time towards leisure activities requires the combination of information taken from two sources; time-use surveys on one hand, and data extracted from satisfaction surveys on the other hand (Krueger *et al.*, 2008). In these surveys respondents rank their levels of satisfaction with the accomplishment of specific activities according to various evaluative criteria. Figure 2.9 illustrates the variations in the ranking of activities depending on whether respondents are asked to describe an objective judgement on an achieved activity ("Evaluative judgement") or to describe their subjective feelings while they are still engaged in the particular activity ("Momentary data capture"). Both the data and the survey focus on the United States, which makes it unclear to which extent other OECD countries follow similar patterns.

It is clear from the measures presented above that some activities like relaxing and socialising after work are much more enjoyed than commuting. Not surprisingly, activities more strongly related to leisure, namely watching television, eating meals (although the time-use approach traditionally categorises eating meals as personal care), relaxing, and

Figure 2.12. **Leisure-related activities are more enjoyed than work-related activities (United States)**

Ranking of activities in decreasing order of average momentary enjoyment

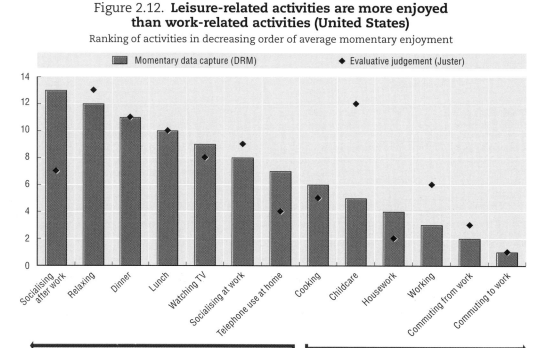

Note: The approach presented above builds on Juster's (1985; p. 333) seminal observation that "an important ingredient in the production and distribution of well-being is the set of satisfactions generated by activities themselves." To assess the satisfactions generated by activities, Juster asked respondents to rate on a scale from 0 to 10 how much they generally enjoyed a type of activity, such as their job or taking care of their children. Later research found that such general enjoyment ratings can deviate in important and theoretically meaningful ways from episodic ratings that pertain to specific instances of the activity. To overcome this problem, Krueger *et al.* use a time diary method more closely connected to the recalled emotional experiences of a day's actual events and circumstances, the DRM. The Day Reconstruction Method (DRM) is a paper-and-pencil questionnaire that first collects time diary information from individuals for the preceding day. For each noted episode, individuals indicate the nature of the activity, who was present, and the extent to which various emotions were present or absent. Individuals describe their emotional state during each episode in terms of intensity ratings on several dimensions of feelings, some of which are positive (*e.g.*, "Happy", "Enjoy myself", "Friendly") and some of which are negative (*e.g.*, "Depressed", "Angry", "Frustrated"). Hence, the DRM combines elements of experience sampling and time diaries, and is designed specifically to facilitate accurate emotional recall.

Source: OECD calculations from data in Krueger *et al.* (2008).

StatLink ⊞⯑⯑ http://dx.doi.org/10.1787/548756102110

socialising with colleagues, are consistently reported as highly enjoyable in terms of momentary data. Conversely, all activities directly or indirectly related to work and family obligations rank very low in the scale of momentary enjoyment.

For most activities the rankings vary little when compared to respondents' evaluative judgements. The one which sticks out is childcare, which is more enjoyed as an evaluative judgment than at the time. Work also possesses similar but less pronounced characteristics. Some activities, such as socialising after work or housework, also show large discrepancies. However, they relatively are more enjoyed at the time than in terms of retrospective evaluative judgement.

Leisure time compared to measures of life satisfaction and market income

A further interesting aspect of leisure is the extent to which leisure time correlates with other measures of well-being at a country level. To address this question two proxy measures of global well-being are compared to two measures of leisure time. The two measures of well-being chosen are a traditional market income measure (in this case net national income per capita – NNI) and a subjective well-being measures (the *Gallup World Poll* 2006 life-satisfaction data). The two main measures of leisure considered are the residual measure, calculated by simply subtracting annual hours worked from total annual hours, and the broad time-use measure.

Figures 2.13 and 2.14 show that average country levels of life satisfaction are reasonably positively correlated to leisure time, whether residual or actual. Countries who sustain much lower levels in life satisfaction given their levels of residual leisure include Hungary, Portugal and Slovakia. On the other hand, given their amounts of leisure, the United States and Australia do remarkably well. Concerning time-use measures of leisure, despite relatively low amounts of leisure, Australians (again) seem satisfied with their lives. Given their time-use measure of leisure, Poland, Turkey and Korea have particularly low levels of life satisfaction.

Figure 2.13. **Residual of paid work time is positively correlated with life satisfaction**

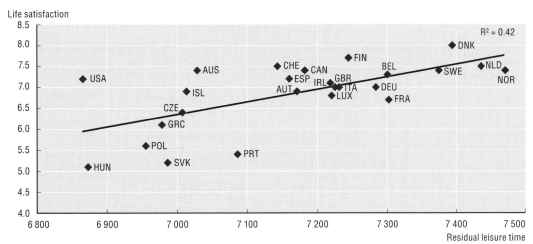

Source: Data from the 2006 Gallup Life-satisfaction Survey and other OECD data. Secretariat estimates based on European Labour Force Surveys results and EIRO (2006 where available).

StatLink ⬛ *http://dx.doi.org/10.1787/548761055333*

Figure 2.14. **Broad leisure time is positively correlated with life satisfaction**

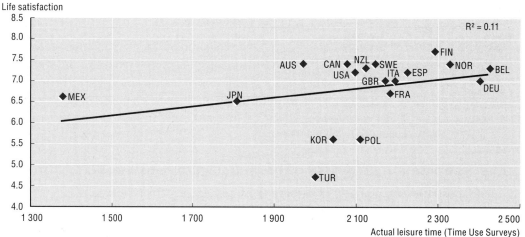

Source: Data from the 2006 Gallup Life-satisfaction Survey and other OECD data. Secretariat estimates based on national and multinational time-use surveys (2006 where available).

StatLink ᴹˢᴾ http://dx.doi.org/10.1787/548770544734

Turning to more traditional market-income based measures of well-being, Figures 2.15 and 2.16 show the positive correlation between leisure time and per capita net national income levels. Again, the correlation is positive for both residual and actual leisure time, a result that suggests that leisure possesses the characteristics of a normal good: more is demanded as incomes rise.

Figure 2.15. **Residual of paid work time is positively correlated to per capita NNI**

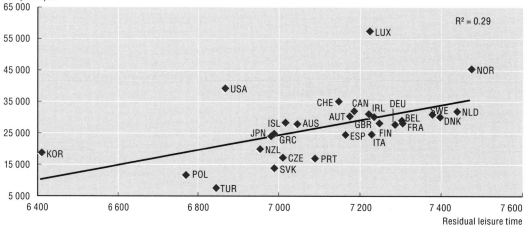

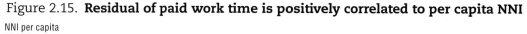

Note: Australia, Japan, Korea, New Zealand, Poland, and Turkey use 2005 data.

Source: Secretariat estimates based on *OECD Annual National Accounts* and *Social Expenditure database* (2006 where available), data from the 2006 Gallup Life-satisfaction Survey, the European Labour Force Surveys results, and EIRO (2006 where available).

StatLink ᴹˢᴾ http://dx.doi.org/10.1787/548775647222

Mandatory holidays and leisure time

Of larger policy interest is the relationship between statutory minimum paid vacations and paid holidays and the amounts of leisure time (whether residual or derived from time-use measures). The primary aim of public regulation of paid holidays is to presumably increase the amount of available leisure time, as well as to coordinate society so families

Figure 2.16. **Broad leisure time is positively correlated with per capita NNI**

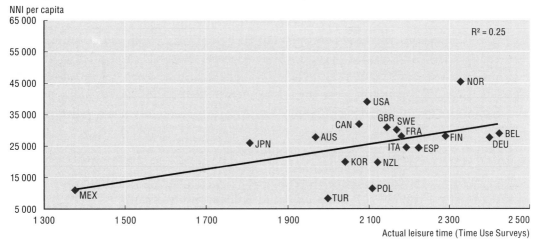

Note: Australia, New Zealand, and Poland use 2005 data. NNI data for Mexico is not available from 2005 onwards. It has been estimated for 2006 using the 2006-04 growth on GDP per capita.

Source: Secretariat estimates based on national and multinational time-use surveys (2006 where available). *OECD Annual National Accounts and Social Expenditure database* (2006 where available). Secretariat estimates based on European Labour Force Surveys results and EIRO (2006 where available).

StatLink ⚞🔗⚟ http://dx.doi.org/10.1787/548783364748

and friends can more readily share their leisure together. Across OECD countries, considerable variations exist in the number of mandatory paid annual leave and paid public holidays; from none in the United States to nearly 10% of the year in Austria, Portugal, and Spain (Figure 2.17).[6]

Figure 2.17. **Paid annual leave and paid public holidays in the OECD**

Annual leave and paid public holidays, days per year

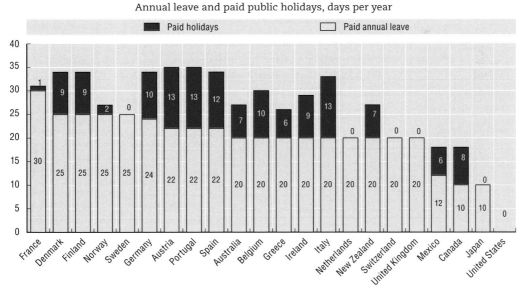

Note: Several nations' laws refer to workdays, while others refer to calendar days or weeks. The comparison assumes a five-day work week. The United States is the only country in the group that does not legally require employers to provide any paid annual leave. Of course, many employers in the countries in Figure 2.17 offer more paid leave and public holidays than the legal minimums described, on the basis of collective and/or individual agreements. This factor is especially important in the United States given that the law does not establish a legal minimum for either kind of benefit. United States law makes no provisions for paid public holidays, as is also the case in Japan, the Netherlands, Sweden, and the United Kingdom. For further information, see source.

Source: Schmitt and Ray (2007), with the exception of Mexico, which is an OECD Secretariat-collected figure.

StatLink ⚞🔗⚟ http://dx.doi.org/10.1787/548802823410

While these policy discrepancies may explain differences in national levels of leisure, it is not clear whether people in a country where legislation guarantees a certain minimum of paid leave and/or public holidays automatically enjoy more leisure. Figure 2.18 shows that there is a positive correlation between levels of total annual leave (paid annual leave plus paid holidays) and residual leisure, which suggests that policies regulating holidays might be relatively successful. Additionally, when total annual leave is compared to the superior time-use measures of leisure in Figure 2.19 for the OECD18, the positive relationship still exists and indeed is somewhat stronger. Regulatory policy regarding paid holidays may be able to influence the amount of leisure that people have, although there are obvious cautions about necessarily reading a causal effect into the correlation.

Figure 2.18. **The relationship between residual of paid work time and regulated paid leave is reasonably strong**

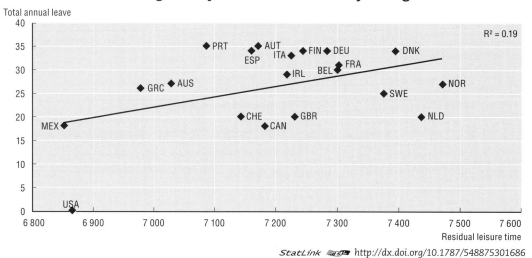

StatLink ⬛ http://dx.doi.org/10.1787/548875301686

Figure 2.19. **The relationship between broad leisure time and regulated paid leave is stronger**

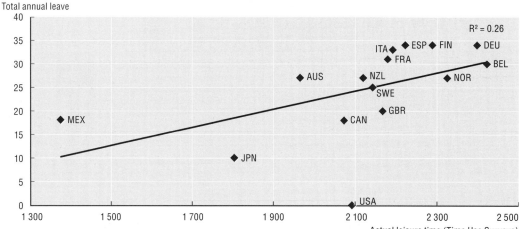

Note: Several nations' laws refer to workdays, while others refer to calendar days or weeks. The comparison assumes a five-day workweek.

Source: Schmitt and Ray (2007) and Secretariat estimates based on national and multinational time-use surveys (2006 where available).

StatLink ⬛ http://dx.doi.org/10.1787/548881462071

Conclusion

This chapter has explored the ways in which leisure differs between and within OECD countries, as well as across time. Attention was paid to the conceptual issues related to the empirical measurement of leisure, opening the analysis with an intentionally simplistic initial definition of leisure as "time not worked" in order to progressively enrich it *via* comparable data extracted from time-use surveys. A particular point of focus was the malleability of leisure levels and trends when using different definitions of "leisure" (broader and narrower definitions). A major conclusion of this chapter is that when it comes to analysing difficult notions such as "leisure", conceptual definitions are extremely important and may change overall country rankings and some socio-demographic patterns.

Data from time-use surveys help monitor the actual living conditions of OECD populations. These statistics make it possible to observe the lifestyles of various groups and their choices of certain activities over others, as well as to improve the interpretation and the understanding of various social and economic phenomena. As such, they can be of great use to government agencies, particularly those involved in advising on, implementing, and monitoring public policy (Callister, 2004).

Policy makers typically consider social policies in terms of efficiency and equity. Leisure-related policies should be no different. Policy choices currently influence leisure time in ways that are both direct and subtle. Most importantly, the work/non-work margin, and thus the maximum amount of time available for leisure is affected by levels of disposable income (through income effects) and marginal effective tax rates (influencing the substitution of work for non-work). More generally the panoply of policies affecting labour supply, ranging from child- and out-of-school care provision to public subsidies to higher education, matters for the paid work/non-work choice. In addition to the tax-benefit system, both labour market and product market regulation are designed to affect the amounts of available leisure in OECD countries. Concerning the labour market, public holidays and minimum annual holidays are frequently regulated. Concerning the product market, shopping hours and trading days are also regulated in order to improve people's leisure opportunities. Whether such policies influence the objectives they were designed for in the desired fashion remains an open question.

International comparisons of leisure time using time use studies covering a wide number of countries are still in their infancy. In this context, some sort of OECD-wide repository of time use surveys may allow researchers to improve their comparisons of leisure time between and within member countries. This may be the next most obvious step in order to better understand leisure at a comparative OECD level, encouraging the members who do not currently have such a survey to consider participating in regular internationally-comparable time use surveys.

Notes

1. A comparison of time-use by income level would have been of considerable interest. There was insufficient standardisation in income measures across countries to attempt such an investigation.

2. See also Engler and Staubli (2008) for a more recent and more detailed analysis of leisure through time, which includes adjustments for changing ages, education distributions of the population, and changes in the numbers of children. The authors use data from the same five countries used

here but over a 25-year time period. A major conclusion of their study is that over this period countries have been converging in their leisure time.

3. This finding is at odds with the results of Burda *et al.* (2007), who emphasise on effective gender leisure equality across rich countries. This conclusion is also at odds with another recently published study by Engler and Staubli (2008) who report gender differences in leisure measured by time-use surveys for Canada, the Netherlands, Norway, the United Kingdom and the United States. They find that in fact there is a female advantage in weekly leisure time for all of these five countries. Their study uses two definitions of the concept of "leisure". The first definition is a residual after both paid work (including commuting time) and unpaid work have been subtracted from total time. The second leisure measure subtracts time in education, receiving personal services, religious/community/voluntary activities, and adds gardening time.

4. Engler and Staubli (2008) report much higher shopping times (in excess of two hours per week more) than Burda *et al.* (2007) for both men and women in the United States compared to other countries.

5. The fact that New Zealand, culturally similar to Australia, has amounts of leisure time spent visiting friends and family more like Turkey, suggests there may be comparability issues with the data on types of leisure activities.

6. The main difference between legally mandated annual leave and public holidays is that there is typically some temporal discretion about when the former can be taken, whereas the dates of public holidays are typically fixed. Additionally, with the cyclicity of the calendar, public holidays may from time to time fall on weekends and then, at least in some countries, do not constitute days off work if weekends are not typically worked.

References

Aguiar, M. and E. Hurst (2006), "Measuring Trends in Leisure: The Allocation of Time Over Five Decades", National Bureau of Economic Research, Working Paper No. 12082, Cambridge MA, March.

Aliaga, C. and K. Winqvist (2003), "How Women and Men Spend their Time", *Statistics in Focus: Population and Social Conditions*, Eurostat, Luxembourg.

Apps, P.F. (2003), "Gender, Time Use and Models of the Household", IZA Discussion Paper No. 796, Institute for the Study of Labor, Bonn, June.

Apps, P.F. and R. Rees (1996), "Labour Supply, Household Production and Intra-family Welfare Distribution", *Journal of Public Economics*, Vol. 60, pp. 199-209.

Apps, P.F. and R. Rees (1997), "Collective Labour Supply and Household Production", *Journal of Political Economy*, Vol. 105, pp. 178-190.

Apps, P.F. and R. Rees (2002), "Household Production, Full Consumption and the Costs of Children", *Labour Economics*, Vol. 8, pp. 621-648.

Biddle, J. and D. Hamermesh (1990), "Sleep and the Allocation of Time", *Journal of Political Economy*, Vol. 98, No. 5, pp. 922-943.

Burda, M.C., D.S. Hamermesh and P. Weil (2007), "Total Work, Gender, and Social Norms", IZA Discussion Paper No. 2705, Institute for the Study of Labor, Bonn, March.

Callister, P. (2004), "Time-Use Data and Work-Life Policy Development", *Social Policy Journal of New Zealand*, No. 22, July.

Causa, O. (2008), "Explaining Differences in Hours Worked among OECD Countries: An Empirical Analysis", *OECD Economics Department Working Papers*, No. 596, OECD, Paris.

Chiappori, A. (1997), "Introducing Household Production in Collective Models of Labour Supply", *Journal of Political Economy*, Vol. 105, No. 1, pp. 191-209.

Engler, M. and S. Staubli (2008), "The Distribution of Leisure Time across Countries and Over Time", Department of Economics Discussion Paper No. 2008-14, University of St. Gallen, Switzerland.

Gronau, R. (1976), "Leisure, Home Production and Work – The Theory of the Allocation of Time Revisited", NBER Working Paper No. 137, Cambridge, MA, May.

Koreman, P. and A. Kapteyn (1987), "A Disaggregated Analysis of the Allocation of Time within the Household", *Journal of Political Economy*, Vol. 95, No. 2, pp. 223-249.

Krueger, A.B., D. Kahneman and D. Schkade (2008), "National Time Accounting: The Currency of Life", third draft of unpublished paper, March 31.

Parnanen, A., H. Sutela and S. Mahler (2005), *Combining Family and Full-Time Work*, European Foundation for the Improvement of Living and Working Conditions, Report No. TN0510TR02, Dublin.

Ramey, V.A. and F. Neville (2006), "A Century of Work and Leisure", NBER Working Paper No. 12264, Cambridge, MA, May.

Schmitt, J. and R. Ray (2007), *No Vacation Nation USA – A Comparison of Leave and Holiday in OECD Countries*, Center for Economic and Policy Research, European Economic and Employment Policy Brief No. 3-2007, Washington, May.

Solberg, E. and D. Wong (1992), "Family Time-use, Home Production, Market Work and Work-Related Travel", *Journal of Human Resources*, Vol. 27, No. 3, pp. 485-510.

Veblen, T. (1899), *The Theory of the Leisure Class*, Penguin Classics.

ANNEX 2.A1

Main Features of Time-Use Surveys

This annex describes some of the characteristics of time-use surveys identified by the OECD Secretariat as suitable for inclusion in the chapter.

Context

Time-use surveys are the primary statistical vehicle for recording information on how people precisely allocate their time across different day-to-day activities. The surveys consist mainly in a large number of people keeping a diary of activities over one or several representative days for a given period. Respondents describe the activities in which they engaged, and these are then re-coded by national statistical agencies into a set of descriptive categories. A well-designed survey classifies activities across a total duration of 24 hours a day (or 1 440 minutes).

Interest in time-use studies has grown considerably over the last 20 years. A number of national statistical agencies have conducted large-scale time-use surveys in recent decades).

Most time-use data sets are large enough to generate reliable measures of time allocation over the full year, but the accuracy of these estimates varies significantly from country to country. Differences in survey features, number of diary days sampled, and categorisation of activities used may affect the cross-country comparability of results.

The most important dimensions in which time-use surveys differ are the following:

- **Sample design.** All time-use surveys included in this chapter are based on nationally-representative samples of resident non-institutionalised populations. National surveys differ, however, in terms of sample design, with some surveys relying on a random sample and others using a pre-established sample taken from other large-scale population surveys. Time-use surveys also differ in terms of sample size (from around 4 000 to about 200 000 people), age of respondents included in the sample (usually those aged 15 and over, but with several exceptions) and response rates (because of the large non-response rates, some surveys reweight the actual number of completed time-use diaries in order to take into account potential non-respondents). Time-use survey also differ in terms of information on the demographic characteristics that are collected, in how these characteristics are defined (e.g. labour force status), and in terms of the contextual information provided for each activity (e.g. where they were performed, whether additional people were present at that time, etc.).

- **Activity classification.** All surveys classify the respondents' verbal and/or written descriptions of their activities into a set of broader categories. While these coding systems vary according to the survey's goals and ambitions, they lead to classifications with different degrees of detail.* Differences in categorisation stem mainly from choices made to allocate certain activities into broader categories. For instance, some surveys regroup all purchasing activities into one "shopping" category, while some differentiate according to the purpose of the purchases (*i.e.* purchasing groceries, office supplies, household objects/services, etc.). Some surveys categorise sports and volunteer activities into a broad "socialising and leisure" category, while others separate individual leisure activities (computer-gaming) from collective leisure activities (participating in a sports match). Some surveys include civic and religious activities under "other activities" while others omit them entirely. Some surveys include the time spent responding to the survey, while others do not. Finally, some surveys include a separate category for time spent travelling, sometimes divided according to the purpose of the travelling (*i.e.* travelling to and from work will be in the "work-related activities" category, and travelling for a holiday will be in the "socialising and leisure" category) while other include such types of travelling time in the broader category to which they pertain.

- **Number of diary days.** Different methodological choices are made in order to determine the number of diary days to be completed by each participant. For example, the United States survey (ATUS) asks each respondent to complete a time diary for only one day, but most surveys typically obtain data for two days. Both options have their pros and cons. The time spent on various activities on any particular day may not be representative of how respondents typically spend their time, although such anomalies should average out across the full sample of respondents. Conversely, time-budget information for several days allows addressing issues related to how activities are combined over several days, although this comes at the cost of depressing response rates. In general, the relative value of having multiple reports from each particular respondent as opposed to single reports from a larger number of respondents depends on the general objective of the survey.

- **Period over which the survey is conducted.** Time-use responses are generally representative of activities in which people engage on the days of the week for which they complete time budgets. These estimates, however, may not be representative of the full year. As such, time-use surveys differ in terms of the period covered by each survey. For instance the United States survey is spread over the whole year and provides accurate estimates for the full year. Others cover particular periods in the year, which are typically chosen to avoid seasonal biases such as those due to public holidays or annual leave for workers. For some countries, however, the period of field work may not be representative of the full year. The different choices made with respect to the period of field work typically depend on the goals of the survey, on the practical capabilities of statistical institutes, and the availability of financial resources.

---

* The American Time-use Survey (ATUS), for example, begins with a three-tier six-digit coding system out of which basic codes are aggregated into 17 top-level categories: 1) Personal care activities (mainly sleep); 2) Household activities; 3) Caring for and helping household members; 4) Caring for and helping non-household members; 5) Work and work-related activities; 6) Education; 7) Consumer purchases (*e.g.* food shopping); 8) Purchasing professional and personal care services (*e.g.* doctors' visits); 9) Purchasing household services; 10) Obtaining government services and civic obligations; 11) Eating and drinking; 12) Socializing, relaxing, and leisure; 13) Sports, exercise, and recreation; 14) Religious and spiritual activities; 15) Volunteer activities; 16) Telephone calls; and 17) Travelling.

- **Recording of secondary activities.** Surveys also differ in how and if they record activities that are performed simultaneously. Generally, the data are coded as to show people engaged in one activity at a time. In some cases, however, surveys include separate questions designed to learn about simultaneous activities (*i.e.* watching television while cooking, or caring for children while performing other types of occupations), which allows a distinction between "primary" and "secondary" activities. Even when collecting information on simultaneous activities, most statistical institutes ensure uniformity in the coding of respondents' descriptions of their primary activities and then create a more detailed set of basic codes for sub-categories. One limitation of the data produced in this way is that "primary" activities are meticulously tracked while "secondary" ones are usually overlooked. A further element affecting the comparability of estimates for secondary activities is whether activities that typically require only a few minutes of one's time – for instance moving a load of laundry from the washer to the dryer – are reported consistently enough to produce comparable estimates of time devoted to them. Because of the omission of secondary activities, the amount of time devoted to specific tasks that may be performed simultaneously with other tasks is typically under-reported.

- **Recording of activities by spouses.** National surveys also differ in the extent to which information is obtained across different members of the same household. While some surveys record data from one person in each household, others (*e.g.* Australia, Germany and Korea) rely on diaries filled by both spouses in married-couples. Diaries from both spouses shed light on some types of interactions between spouses' uses of time (for example in terms of the combined time devoted by parents to the care of their children), although this information is irrelevant for the purpose of measuring how a population allocates its time. As in other cases, the benefits of this additional information have to be offset against potential costs in terms of response rates and data accuracy.

Table 2.A1.1. **Methodological documentation of national time-use surveys**

	Name of the survey	Agency	Year	Website (data and documentation)	Period of assessment	Population covered	Sample size	Number and type of diary days	Other data features
Australia	Time Use Survey	Australian Bureau of Statistics	2006	www.abs.gov.au/ AUSSTATS/abs@.nsf/ Latestproducts/ 4153.0Main%20Feature s22006?opendocument &tabname=Summary& prodno=4153.0&issue= 2006&num=&view=	Four 13-day periods containing a representative proportion of public holidays and school holidays	People aged 15 years and over living in private dwellings (excluding people living in very remote and non-private dwellings, households containing non-Australians and indigenous communities)	About 3 900 households	Diary for two separate days, with fixed intervals of five minutes	Information obtained partly by interviews and partly by self-completion diary Classification into primary and secondary activities, for whom the activity is done, who else is present and where the activity takes place
Belgium	Harmonised European Time Use Survey (HETUS)	Eurostat and NSO	2005	www.testh2.scb.se/tus/ tus/	One year	Two survey populations are considered: Individuals aged 12 years old or older belonging to the Belgian population and living in private households	35 000 households in the initial sample (before non-responses)	Each respondent fills in diaries for two diary days each covering 24 hours	Short, random moments in people's lives are studied and thus cannot be regarded as representative
Canada	General Social Survey (special module)	Statistics Canada	2005	http:// cansim2.statcan.ca/cgi-win/ cnsmcgi.exe?Lang=E& RootDir=CII/ &ResultTemplate=CII/ CII_pick&Array_Pick=1 &ArrayId=1130001	11 monthly samples of equal size from January to November (extended to mid-December)	Non-institutionalised persons aged 15 years and over living in Canadian provinces, excluding people without telephones (2% of the population) and owning only a cellular telephone (about 5%)	About 25 000 individuals	Computer assisted telephone interviewing (CATI)	Sub-samples fill special modules on "Culture, Sports and Physical Activity Participation", "Social Network and Trust" and "transportation"
Finland	Harmonised European Time Use Survey (HETUS)	Eurostat and NSO	1998	www.testh2.scb.se/tus/ tus/	One year	Individuals aged 10 and over living in private households and all household members	4 800 households containing 12 512 individuals of whom 10 978 are aged ten or over	Each respondent fills in diaries for two diary days each covering 24 hours	Short, random moments in people's lives are studied and thus cannot be regarded as representative
France	Harmonised European Time Use Survey (HETUS)	Eurostat and NSO	1998	www.testh2.scb.se/tus/ tus/	One year	Persons aged 15 and over belonging to the household population, excluding people living in institutions	12 045 dwellings out of which 10 330 are retained in the final sample, representing 16 462 eligible persons	Each respondent fills in diaries for two diary days each covering 24 hours	Short, random moments in people's lives are studied and thus cannot be regarded as representative
Germany	Harmonised European Time Use Survey (HETUS)	Eurostat and NSO	2002	www.testh2.scb.se/tus/ tus/	One year	All private households including individuals aged 10 and older excluding persons without a fixed abode and individuals living in group quarters and similar institutions (military barracks, institutions for the retired, etc.)	About 5 443 household in the final sample	Each respondent fills in diaries for two diary days each covering 24 hours	Short, random moments in people's lives are studied and thus cannot be regarded as representative
Italy	Harmonised European Time Use Survey (HETUS)	Eurostat and NSO	2003	www.testh2.scb.se/tus/ tus/	One year	All members of households residing in Italy aged over 3 and including the elderly (no upper age limit)	21 075 households representing 55 760 individuals.	Each respondent fills in diaries for two diary days each covering 24 hours	Short, random moments in people's lives are studied and thus cannot be regarded as representative

Table 2.A1.1. Methodological documentation of national time-use surveys (cont.)

	Name of the survey	Agency	Year	Website (data and documentation)	Period of assessment	Population covered	Sample size	Number and type of diary days	Other data features
Japan	Survey on Time Use and Leisure Activities	Statistics Bureau and Statistical Research Training Institute	2006	www.stat.go.jp/English/data/shakai/	Two consecutive days from 14 to 22 October 2006	All persons aged 10 and over including foreigners living in Japan	80 000 households, representing around 200 000 people	Two questionnaires: Questionnaire A adopts a pre-coding method and Questionnaire B is probes more detailed time use	Schedules for recording time use for each quarter hour are distributed to the respondents
Korea	Time Use Survey	Korea National Statistical Office	2004	www.nso.go.kr/eng2006/e02__0000/e02c_0000/e02cb_0000/e02cb_0000.html	12 days from September 2 to September 13	Individuals aged 10 years and over	About 12 750 households	Diary for all household members aged 10 years and over (recording of main and simultaneous activities, structured around 10 minutes intervals for the designated two days)	The sample frame is generated from the multi-purpose household sample (HAF-MP) which is derived from the 2000 Population and Housing Census
Mexico	National Survey on Time Use (Encuesta Nacional sobre Uso del Tiempo, ENUT)	Instituto Nacional de Estadística, Geografía e Informática (INEGI)	2002	www.inegi.gob.mx/est/contenidos/espanol/proyectos/metadatos/encuestas/enut_2310.asp?s=est&c=5440	28 days comprised of 4 rounds of 7 days each	National households residing regularly in private living quarters in the national territory	5 450 households actually visited and interviewed		ENUT is a module of the National Survey of Household Income and Expenses (Encuesta Nacional de Ingresos y Gastos de los Hogares, ENIGH)
New Zealand	Time Use Survey (TUS)	Statistics New Zealand (SNZ)	1999 (one off)	www2.stats.govt.nz/domino/external/omni/omni.nsf/outputs/Time+Use+Survey	Between July 1998 and June 1999	All non-institutionalised civilians aged 12 years and over residing in private households	7 200 selected households with a total expected sample size of approximately 8 500 people	Data focuses on the four basic categories of time (contracted time, committed time, necessary time, and free time)	
Norway	Harmonised European Time Use Survey (HETUS)	Eurostat and NSO	2001	www.testh2.scb.se/tus/tus/	One year	All individuals aged 9-79 years (with an extra sample of 60-66-year-olds) and registered in Norway	Main sample of 6 470 individuals	Each respondent fills in diaries for two diary days each covering 24 hours	Short, random moments in people's lives are studied and thus cannot be regarded as representative
Poland	Harmonised European Time Use Survey (HETUS)	Eurostat and NSO	2004 (one-off)	www.testh2.scb.se/tus/tus/	One year	Individuals aged 15 or over with members of the selected households representing six socio-economic groups	10 256 selected households	Each respondent fills in diaries for two diary days each covering 24 hours	One weekday and one weekend day (Saturday or Sunday), preceding or following the weekday, is assigned on random selection basis to each dwelling in the main sample

Table 2.A1.1. Methodological documentation of national time-use surveys (cont.)

	Name of the survey	Agency	Year	Website (data and documentation)	Period of assessment	Population covered	Sample size	Number and type of diary days	Other data features
Spain	Harmonised European Time Use Survey (HETUS)	Eurostat and NSO	2003	www.testh2.scb.se/tus/ tus/	One year	All members aged 10 or older of regular resident households	20 603 households representing 46 774 individuals	Each respondent fills in diaries for two diary days each covering 24 hours	All days of the year are covered
Sweden	Harmonised European Time Use Survey (HETUS)	Eurostat and NSO	2001	www.testh2.scb.se/tus/ tus/	One year	Individuals aged 20-84 registered in Sweden during the survey period	2 138 households representing 3 980 individuals	Each respondent fills in diaries for two diary days each covering 24 hours	The household sample is constructed by taking a sample of individuals and joining a partner to the selected individual, which means that we do not know how many individuals the household sample contained, only how many individuals there were in the response set
Turkey	Time Use Survey	Turkish Statistical Institute (Turkstat)	2006	www.turkstat.gov.tr/ PreHaberBultenleri.do?i d=528	One year	Members of households aged 15 years and over	5 070 selected households, out of which 11 815 members of households aged 15 years and over are interviewed.	Two diaries: one for a weekday and one for a weekend day, daily activities recorded during 24 hours at ten-minute- slots	
United Kingdom	Harmonised European Time Use Survey (HETUS)	Eurostat and NSO	2001	www.testh2.scb.se/tus/ tus/	From June 2000 to July 2001	All members aged 8 and over in a selected household (Though the final database includes only persons aged 10 and over)	11 854 sampled households resulting in 20 991 diaries	Each respondent fills wo diary days each covering 24 hours	Short, random moments in people's lives are studied and thus cannot be regarded as representative
United States	American Time Use Survey (ATUS)	Bureau of Labor Statistics (BLS)	2005	www.bls.gov/tus/	Full calendar year	People aged 15 and over living in private households	About 13 000 people	Designated persons are pre-assigned a day of the week on which activities are reported. 25 % of the sample is assigned a weekend day	Reporting days are pre-assigned to eliminate biases that might exist if respondents report at their convenience
Multinational	Multinational Time Use Survey (MTUS)	Centre for Time Use Research	2006	www.timeuse.org/mtus/	One year	Population aged 20 to 59 years old		Each entry is built around 7-day diaries for which averages are calculated	The MTUS dataset is comprised of some 20 countries and is regularly expanded

ISBN 978-92-64-04938-3
Society at a Glance 2009
OECD Social Indicators
© OECD 2009

Chapter 3

Interpreting OECD Social Indicators

The purpose of social indicators

Society at a Glance 2009 contributes to addressing two questions:

- Compared with their own past and with other OECD countries, what progress have countries made in their social development?

- How effective have been the actions of society in furthering social development?

Addressing the first societal progress question requires indicators covering a broad range of social outcomes across countries and time. As social development requires improvements in health, education, and economic resources, as well as a stable basis for social interactions, indicators have to be found for all these dimensions.

The second societal effectiveness question is even more challenging to answer. Societies try to influence social outcomes, often through government policy. A critical issue is whether policies are effective in achieving their aims. Indicators help in making that assessment. A first step is to compare the resources intended to change outcomes across countries and contrast these resources with social outcomes. While this comparison is far from a comprehensive evaluation of policy effectiveness, indicators can contribute to highlighting areas where more evaluative work may be needed.

The framework of OECD social indicators

The structure applied here is not a full-scale social indicators framework. But it is more than a simple indicator list. This framework has been informed by experiences in other parts of the OECD on policy and outcome assessment in a variety of fields. It draws, in particular, on the OECD experience with environmental indicators. These indicators are organised in a framework known as "Pressure-State-Response" (PSR).* In this framework human activities exert *pressures* on the environment, which affect natural resources and environmental conditions (*state*), and which prompt society to respond to these changes through various policies (*societal response*). The PSR framework highlights these sequential links which in turn helps decision-makers and the public see often over-looked interconnections.

A similar approach for social indicators is followed in this report. Indicators are grouped along two dimensions. The first dimension considers the *nature* of these indicators, grouping them in three areas:

- **Social context** refers to variables that, while not usually direct policy targets, are crucial for understanding the social policy context. For example, the proportion of elderly people in the total population is not a policy target. However, it is relevant information on the social landscape in which, for example, health, taxation or pension policy

---

* The PSR framework is itself a variant of an approach which has also given rise to the "Driving force-State-Response" (DSR) model used by the United Nations Committee for Sustainable Development; and the "Driving force-Pressure-State-Impact-Response" (DPSIR) model used by the European Environment Agency.

responses are made. Unlike other indicators, trends in social context indicators cannot be unambiguously interpreted as "good" or "bad".

● **Social status** indicators describe the social outcomes that policies try to influence. These indicators describe the general conditions of the population. Ideally, the indicators chosen are ones that can be easily and unambiguously interpreted – all countries would rather have low poverty rates than high ones, for example.

● **Societal response** indicators provide information about what society is doing to affect social status indicators. Societal responses include indicators of government policy settings. Additionally activities of non-governmental organisations, families and broader civil society are also societal responses. By comparing societal response indicators with social status indicators, one can get an initial indication of policy effectiveness.

While social indicators are allocated to one of the three groups above, the allocation between context and status categories is not always straightforward. For example, fertility rates may be an objective of pro-natalist policies in countries such as France. In other countries, like the United Kingdom, they are part of the context of social policy. Similarly, family breakdown can be regarded as a failure of public policies in some countries, whereas it may not be an explicit policy concern in others.

An important limitation of social context, social status and social response indicators used here is that in this report these are presented at a national level. For member countries with a significant degree of federalism, such as the United States, Canada and Australia, indicators may not be reflective of the regions within the federation, who may have different contexts, outcomes and social responses. This limitation should be borne in mind in considering the indicators presented below.

The second dimension of the OECD framework groups indicators according to the broad policy fields that they cover. Four broad *objectives* of social policy are used to classify indicators of *social status* and *social response*:

● **Self-sufficiency** is an underlying objective of social policy. It features prominently in, for example, the communiqués of O ECD Social and Health Policy Ministers (*www.oecd.org/socmin2005*). Self-sufficiency is promoted by ensuring active social and economic participation by people, and their autonomy in activities of daily life.

● **Equity** is another longstanding objective of social policy. Equitable outcomes are measured mainly in terms of access by people and families to resources.

● **Health status** is a fundamental objective of health care systems, but improving health status also requires a wider focus on its social determinants, making health a central objective of social policy.

● **Social cohesion** is often identified as an over-arching objective of countries' social policies. While little agreement exists on what it means, a range of symptoms are informative about *lack* of social cohesion. Social cohesion is more positively evident in the extent to which people participate in their communities.

The framework behind the OECD social indicators can be represented as a summary "matrix" (Table 3.1). Table 3.1 additionally provides information of the range of social indicators covered by previous editions of *Society at a Glance*, as well as coverage of the current publication.

Table 3.1. Social indicators included in the five editions of Society at a Glance (2001, 2003, 2005, 2006, 2009)

Nature	Content: Self-sufficiency (SS)	Equity (EQ)	Health (HE)	Social cohesion (CO)
Social context	• *National income* • *Migration* • Fertility rates (2001, 2005, 2006, 2009) • Marriage and divorce (2001, 2005, 2006, 2009) • Age-dependency ratio (2001, 2003, 2005, 2006) • Refugees and asylum-seekers (2001) • Sole parents (2001)			
Social status	*Employment* • *Unemployment* • Mothers in paid employment (2001, 2003, 2005, 2006) • Jobless households (2001, 2003, 2005, 2006) • Student performance (2001, 2003, 2005, 2009) • Not in employment, education or training (2001, 2005, 2009) • Age of labour force exit (2001, 2005, 2009) • Childcare costs (2006) • Childcare (2001, 2009)	• Income inequality (2001, 2005, 2009) • Poverty (2001, 2005, 2009) • Poverty among children (2005, 2009) • Income of older people (2003, 2005) • Low paid employment(2001) • Gender wage gaps (2001, 2006) • Material deprivation (2006) • Poverty persistence (2006) • Intergenerational mobility (2006) • Housing costs (2006)	• Life expectancy (2001, 2005, 2006, 2009) • Health adjusted life expectancy (2003, 2005) • Perceived health status (2009) • Infant mortality (2001, 2005, 2009) • Low birth weight (2003, 2006, 2009) • Obesity (2003, 2009) • Height (2009) • Mental health (2009) • Potential years of life lost (2001, 2003) • Disability-free life expectancy (2001) • Accidents (2001) • Sick related absences from work (2006) • Health inequalities (2006)	*Suicides* • Life satisfaction (2005, 2006, 2009) • Crime victimisation (2001, 2003, 2009) • Work satisfaction (2009) • School bullying (2009) • Risky behaviour (2009) • Social isolation (2001, 2005) • Group membership (2001, 2005) • Teenage births (2003, 2005) • Drug use and related deaths (2001, 2005) • Strikes and lockouts (2001, 2003, 2006) • Voting (2001, 2006) • Juvenile crime (2003) • Trust in civil service (2006) • Work accidents (2001, 2006)
Societal responses	*Adequacy of benefits of last resort* • Activation policies (2001) • Spending on education (2001, 2009) • Early childhood education and care (2001) • Literacy among adults (2001) • Tax wedge on labour (2001, 2006) • Students with impairments (2003) • Resources of disabled adults (2002) • Working disabled persons (2003) • Benefits of last resort (2005)	*Public social spending* • *Total social spending* • Private social spending (2001, 2005) • Benefit recipiency (2001, 2005) • Earnings inequality (2006) • Minimum wages (2001) • Pension replacement rate (2006, 2005) • Pension promise (2005)	*Health care expenditure* • Responsibility for financing health care (2003, 2001) • Long-term care recipients (2001, 2005, 2006, 2009) • Health care infrastructure (2001)	• Prisoners (2001, 2003)

Data refer to the domains covered in *Society at a Glance*. Indicators in italics have been included in all five editions. Names shown for each domain of indicators are those used in 2009 edition; some of the indicators may also have been moved from one category to another.

The selection and description of indicators

OECD countries differ substantially in their collection and publication of social indicators. In selecting indicators for this report, the following questions were considered.

● What is the minimum degree of indicator comparability across countries? This report strives to present the best comparative information for each of the areas covered. However the indicators presented are not confined to those for which there is "absolute" comparability. Readers are, however, alerted as to the nature of the data used and the limits to comparability.

● What is the minimum number of countries for which the data must be available? As a general rule, this volume includes only indicators that are available for a majority of OECD countries.

● What breakdowns should be used at a country level? Social indicators can often be decomposed at a national level into outcomes by social sub-categories, such as people's age, gender and family type. Pragmatism governs here: the breakdowns presented here vary according to the indicator considered.

Chapters 4 to 8 of this report describes the key evidence, together with information on definitions and measurement for each of the selected indicators. Most indicators already exist in one form or another. Some are published in other OECD publications on a regular basis (*e.g. Labour Force Statistics, Social Expenditure database, and OECD Health Data*). Others have been collected on an *ad hoc* basis.

Individual indicators can be relevant for multiple areas of social policy. That is to say they could plausibly be included under more than one category. For example, the ability to undertake activities of daily living without assistance is potentially an indicator of social cohesion, self-sufficiency and health. Indicators are presented here under the category for which they are considered primarily most relevant.

Throughout this volume, the code associated with each indicator (*e.g.* GE1) is used to relate it to a policy field (as listed in the tables below), while a numbering of the indicators is used to simplify cross-references. While the name and coding of indicators used in this volume may differ from those in previous issues of *Society at a Glance,* an effort is made to assure continuity in the areas covered.

General social context indicators (GE)

When comparing *social status* and *societal response* indicators, it is easy to suggest that one country is doing badly relative to others, or that another is spending a lot of money in a particular area compared with others. It is important to put such statements into a broader context. For example, national income levels vary across OECD countries. If there is any link between income and health, richer countries may have better health conditions than poor ones, irrespectively of societal responses. If the demand for health care services increases with income (as appears to be the case), rich countries may spend more on health care (as a percentage of national income) than poorer countries. These observations do not mean that the indicators of health status and health spending are misleading. They do mean, however, that the general context behind the data should be borne in mind when considering policy implications.

Social context indicators are of relevance in interpreting many indicators included in this publication. This is true of Net National Income per capita (GE1), which has implications for the quality, quantity and nature of the social protection and education that society can afford to provide, but also of fertility rates (GE2), migration (GE3), and marriage and divorce (GE4).

List of general context indicators (GE)

GE1. Net National Income per capita
GE2. Fertility rates
GE3. Migration
GE4. Marriage and divorce

Self-sufficiency (SS)

For many people in the working-age population, paid employment (SS1) is an important means of obtaining money, identity, social interactions and social status. In addition, all social security systems are funded by contributions by paid working people. Hence promoting higher paid employment is a priority for all OECD countries. Being unemployed (SS2) means, despite being available for work, that supporting oneself and one's dependants through work is not always possible. Early foundations matter for children's cognitive and social development which in turn play an important role in future self-sufficiency. The childcare enrolment rate (SS3) indicates something of the extent to which children are covered by centred-based systems of early learning. Student performance (SS4) signals an important dimension of human capital accumulation at the other end of the child life cycle. Good student performance enables longer term self-sufficiency over the future, including in paid employment. Because long term labour market disadvantage is often signalled by early adult disadvantage, a youth inactivity measure can provide information on chances of a successful transition to a self-sufficient working life (SS5).

The societal response to student performance and youth inactivity has often involved design of the structure and incentives in schooling system (hard to summarise by a social indicator), but has also involved heavy public and private expenditure in education (SS7).

The table below lists the indicators of social status and societal response that are most relevant for assessing whether OECD countries have been successful in meeting goals for assuring the self-sufficiency of people and their families.

List of self-sufficiency indicators (SS)

Social status	Societal responses
SS1. Employment	SS7. Spending on education
SS2. Unemployment	
SS3. Childcare	
SS4. Student performance	
SS5. Not in employment, education or training	
SS6. Age at labour force exit	
EQ1. Income inequality	*EQ4. Adequacy of benefits of last resort*
EQ2. Poverty	*EQ5. Public social spending*
EQ3. Poverty among children	*EQ6. Total net social spending*

Note: Indicators in italics are those that, while presented in another sub-section, are also relevant for an assessment of self-sufficiency.

Equity (EQ)

Equity has many dimensions. It includes the ability to access social services and economic opportunities, as well as equity in actual outcomes. Opinions vary widely as to what exactly entails a fair distribution of outcomes or what establishes a just distribution of opportunities. Additionally, as it is hard to obtain information on all dimensions of equity, the *social status* equity indicators are limited to inequality in financial resources.

Income inequality (EQ1) is a natural starting point for considering equity across the whole of society. Often however, policy concerns are more strongly on those at the bottom end of the income distribution. Hence the use of poverty measures (EQ2). Children are often a particular cause for concern, both because of their lack of choice regarding their material circumstances and because of the longer term developmental consequences of being poor. Thus it is of considerable value to include a poverty measure focussing exclusively on children (EQ3).

Social protection systems are a major tool through which policy-makers respond to these equity concerns. All OECD countries have developed (or are developing) social protection systems that, to a varying extent, redistribute resources within societies and insure people against various contingencies. Adequacy of benefits of last resort (EQ4) picks up the policy response to some of the most disadvantaged citizens. These interventions are summarised by public social spending (EQ5). Total net social spending (EQ6) takes into additional consideration tax breaks and income claw backs.

Equity indicators are clearly related to self-sufficiency indicators. Taken together, they reveal how national social protection systems grapple with a recurrent policy dilemma: how to balance adequacy of provisions with sustainability of the system and promotion of citizens' self-sufficiency.

List of equity indicators (EQ)

Social status	Societal responses
EQ1. Income inequality	EQ4. Adequacy of benefits of last resort
EQ2. Poverty	EQ5. Public social spending
EQ3. Poverty among children	EQ6. Total social spending
SS1. Employment	*HE4. Health care expenditure*
SS2. Student performance	
SS3. Unemployment	
HE8. Height	

Note: Indicators in italics are those that, while presented in another sub-section, are also relevant for an assessment of equity outcomes.

Health (HE)

The links between social and health conditions are strong. Indeed, growth in living standards and education, accompanied by better access to health care and continuing progress in medical technology, has contributed to significant improvements in health status, as measured by life expectancy (HE1). Equally important and supplementary to measures of life expectancy are people's self-assessed perceptions of their state of health (HE2). To a significant extent, life expectancy improvements reflect lower infant mortality and improvements in low birth weight as indicators of better infant health (HE3). Obesity (HE4) reduces social and economic functioning and is a forward-looking indicator of health problems and costs. A further indicator of cumulative physical health during childhood which is achieving increasing attention is attained adult height (HE5). Often the focus in the health area is on physical health, with mental health (HE6) often overlooked. This is partly because of measurement and data problems. Yet mental health problems have high personal and societal costs and poor, mental and physical health are often associated.

List of health indicators (HE)

Social status	Societal responses
HE1. Life expectancy	HE7. Long-term care recipients
HE2. Perceived health status	HE8. Health care expenditure
HE3. Infant health	
HE4. Obesity	
HE5. Height	
HE6. Mental health	
CO4. Suicides	EQ4. Adequacy of benefits of last resort
	EQ5. Public social spending
	EQ6. Total social spending

Note: Indicators in italics are those that, while presented in another sub-section, are also relevant for an assessment of health outcomes.

A response to health issues is the provision of different forms of long-term care to the elderly, either in institutions or at home (HE7). Health care expenditure (HE8) is a more general and key part of the policy response of health care systems to concerns about health conditions. Nevertheless, health problems have sometimes their root in interrelated social conditions – such as unemployment, poverty, and inadequate housing – that are outside the reach of health policies. Moreover, more than spending levels *per se*, the effectiveness of health interventions often depends on other characteristics of the health care system, such as low coverage of medical insurance or co-payments, which may act as barriers to seeking medical help. A broader range of indicators on health conditions and interventions is provided in *OECD Heath Data* and in *Health at a Glance*, a biennial companion volume.

Social cohesion (CO)

Promoting social cohesion is an important social policy goal in many OECD countries. However, because there is no commonly-accepted definition, identifying suitable indicators is especially difficult. The approach taken in *Society at a Glance* is to assess social cohesion through indicators that describe the extent to which citizens participate in societal life and derive satisfaction from their daily activities, indicators that inform about various pathologies and conditions that put affected people at risk of social exclusion, or indicators that reveal the extent of social strife.

Survey data on subjective life satisfaction (CO1) provide both important direct measures of people's well-being and of the cohesion in society as a whole. The workplace is an environment where most people spend important parts of their lives. Satisfaction with work (CO2) is thus an important sub-dimension of well-being, an indicator of cohesion in a key environment. Criminal activity is a measure of social breakdown and crime victimisation (CO3) is also likely to erode levels of trust in society, important for social cohesion. Suicide (CO4) can be seen as the ultimate abandonment of society by the individual person, where social bonds are not sufficient to prevent a person taking their own life. For younger members of society, the school is perhaps the most important environment outside the family. Bullying in schools (CO5) is an important negative indicator of social cohesion in the school environment. Another indicator of social cohesion for youth is risky behaviour (CO6). Some risky behaviour is of course normal and, in some directions, a part of growing up. However, societies which lack cohesion across generations may generate undesirably high rates of risky behaviours and in undesirable directions.

Beyond these indicators of social status, context indicators may also help to highlight the existence of different groups and families within society that are exposed to special risk of social exclusion. Finally, it should be noted that it is much more difficult to identify relevant response indicators to social cohesion issues. All of the policies that are relevant to other dimensions of social policy (self-sufficiency, equity and health) may also influence social cohesion.

List of social cohesion indicators (CO)

Social status	Societal responses
CO1. Life satisfaction	
CO2. Work satisfaction	
CO3. Crime victimisation	
CO4. Suicides	
CO5. School bullying	
CO6. Risky behaviour	
SS2. Unemployment	EQ5. Public social spending
EQ1. Income inequality	EQ6. Total social spending
EQ2. Poverty	HE2. Heath care spending
EQ3. Poverty amongst children	
HE7. Mental health	

Note: Indicators in italics are those that, while presented in another sub-section, are also relevant for an assessment of social cohesion outcomes.

What can be found in this publication

For each of the areas covered in Chapters 4 to 8 of this report, an opening boxed section on "Definition and measurement" provides the definition of the relevant indicator(s) and a discussion of measurement issues. In particular, it focuses on inter-country comparability issues. Some of the indicators are not precisely comparable. Where comparability is a potential issue, the box provides this qualitative information. The main discussion follows the Definition and measurement box. Typically this begins with a discussion of cross-country differences, followed by consideration of time trends, for the OECD on average and a selection of interesting country-cases. Demographic and socio-economic breakdowns are explored where possible. Evidence is presented in the form of figures and tables, with selected references for "further reading" and titles of publications from which indicators are derived.

In order to present the key data concisely, this publication does not include all dimensions for all the indicators collected. The data underlying each indicator are available on the OECD website (*www.oecd.org/els/social/indicators/SAG*), or can be accessed via the *StatLinks* for each indicator (where data for additional countries are also available).

4. GENERAL CONTEXT INDICATORS

1. Net national income per capita

2. Fertility rates

3. Migration

4. Marriage and divorce

Definition and measurement

Net national income (NNI) per capita is the best indicator for comparing economic well-being across countries available in the System of National Accounts (SNA). NNI is defined as gross domestic product (GDP) *plus* net receipts of wages, salaries and property income from abroad, *minus* the depreciation of fixed capital assets (dwellings, buildings, machinery, transport equipment and physical infrastructure) through wear and tear and obsolescence. Estimates of NNI per capita, however, are subject to greater uncertainties than those associated to GDP per capita, the most widely used indicator of national income. Uncertainties exist because of difficulties in measuring international income flows and capital depreciation.

For cross-country comparison, national currency measures of NNI are converted into a common metric by using purchasing power parity exchange rates (PPPs). These reflect the amount of a national currency that is required in each country to buy the same basket of goods and services as a United States dollar (USD) does in the United States. Estimates of PPPs are computed by the OECD and Eurostat by comparing the prices of about 2 500 items in different countries (Schreyer and Koechlin, 2002). NNI per capita is obtained by dividing NNI by the size of the resident population, which includes both people living in private households and those in institutions. Both NNI and PPP estimates are affected by statistical errors. Consequently NNI differences between countries of 5% or less are not considered significant.

Average OECD national income per capita was around 26 000 United States dollars in 2006. In that year, three OECD countries had a per capita income in excess of USD 35 000 – Luxembourg, Norway and the United States. Eight countries had a per capita income below USD 20 000 and two (Mexico and Turkey) were around USD 11 000 (GE1.1) (note the Mexican figure is for 2004).

Average NNI per capita in the OECD has increased by 2.6% annually since the new millennium for the 17 countries for which real NNI data are available. (GE1.2). NNI has increased annually by over 5% in the Slovak Republic and by nearly 4.5% in Greece. Annual average Italian and German NNI growth, by contrast, was a modest 1%. There is little relationship evident between growth rates between 2000 and 2006 and NNI levels in 2000.

OECD countries with higher average NNI per capita tend to spend a higher proportion of NNI on social protection. The relation is however not strong, and is generated to a considerable degree by the outlying positions of Mexico, Turkey and Korea (GE1.3). Austria, Denmark, France and Sweden spend more on social expenditure than predicted given their income per capita. Conversely, Mexico, Korea, Turkey and to a lesser extent the United States spend less than predicted. There are a number of possible explanations for this pattern. Some social expenditure buys the services of others – medical or childcare, for example. As the earnings of such service providers increase alongside those of other earners, but without the same productivity growth, social expenditure rises (Arjona *et al.*, 2001). Equally, the services provided by welfare state may be strongly income-responsive compared to other goods and services.

Further reading

Arjona, R., M. Ladaique and M. Pearson (2001), "Growth, Inequality and Social Protection", Labour Market and Social Policy Occasional Paper No. 51, OECD, Paris.

OECD (2008), *National Accounts*, OECD, Paris.

Schreyer, P. and F. Koechlin (2002), "Purchasing Power Parities – Measurement and Uses", *OECD Statistics Brief*, No. 3, OECD, Paris, March.

Figure note

Figure GE1.2: Many countries do not create price deflators for NNI. Therefore data on real NNI growth is limited to 17 countries. NNI: Net national income.

GE1.1. National income per capita of OECD countries varies between USD 11 000 and 55 000

Net national income per capita in current USD using PPPs in 2006, OECD average = USD 26 500

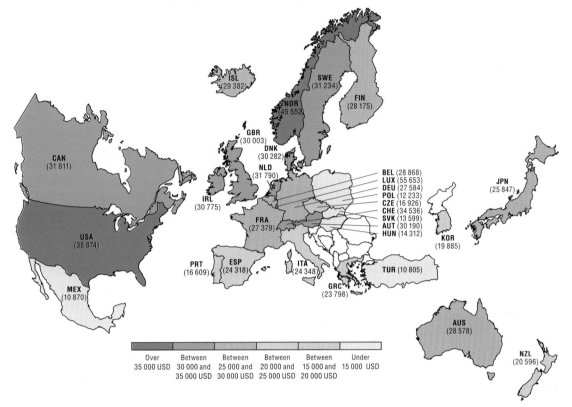

GE1.2. Recent NNI growth varied between 1% and 5% per year

Real annual average growth in NNI per capita between 2000 and 2006, in percentage

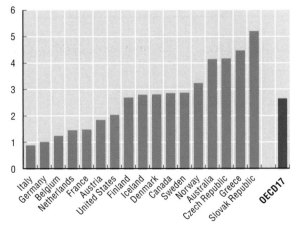

GE1.3. Countries with higher Net National Income have higher proportional public social spending

The share of public social spending in % of NNI and NNI per capita in USD at PPPs, 2005

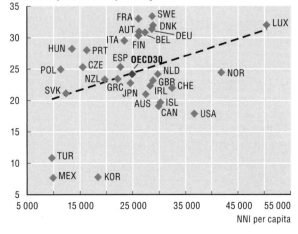

Source: OECD Annual National Accounts (*www.oecd.org/statistics/ national-accounts*) and Social Expenditure database (*www.oecd.org/els/ social/expenditure*).

StatLink http://dx.doi.org/10.1787/550002185115

Definition and measurement

The total fertility rate is the number of children that would be born to each woman at the end of her childbearing years if the likelihood of her giving birth to children at each age was the currently prevailing age-specific fertility rates. It is computed by summing up the age-specific fertility rates defined over five-yearly intervals. Assuming no net migration and unchanged mortality, total fertility rate of 2.1 children per woman ("replacement") ensures broad population stability.

The mean age of mothers at first child birth is computed as the mean of the different ages, weighted by the fertility rate at that age. The share of births outside marriage, is the ratio of the number of live births occurred outside a registered marriage in a year and the total number of living births in the same year.

Data typically come from civil, population registers or other administrative records and are harmonised according to United Nations and Eurostat recommendations. The exception is Turkey, where fertility data are survey-based.

Fertility is low across most of the OECD. Low fertility arises for a variety of reasons. These include changes in lifestyle choices, labour market insecurity, difficulties in finding suitable housing, unaffordable, unavailable or low quality childcare, rising female education levels, reductions in workplace discrimination against women, as well as a failure of policies to provide adequate support to families juggling work and having children. Many of these constraints can explain the long-term decline in fertility rates in OECD countries (D'Addio and Mira d'Ercole, 2005).

Fertility is well below the replacement level in most OECD countries. In 2006, fertility rates averaged 1.65 across OECD countries. The few countries above replacement include Mexico and Turkey (at 2.2) and Iceland and the United States (around 2.1).

Fertility declines can create policy challenges. These include responding to a decline in the availability of family carers in old age, a growing tax burden on those of working age to finance pensions and health care, an older workforce, and a smaller pool of domestic savings.

There has been a moderate recovery in fertility rates from 2002. In 2002 the average OECD rate was 1.60, recovering to 1.65 in 2006 (GE2.1). The recovery occurs for 17 countries, with the biggest increases in the United Kingdom, France, Sweden, Spain, and the Czech Republic. The rebound may be due to an increase of births given by women who have postponed motherhood until their thirties or later (Sardon, 2006). Policy measures, including more support for families and working women, may also have played a role.

Women are having their first child at older ages. The average age of mothers at first childbirth has increased on average by around one year per decade since 1970 (Table GE2.2). Besides contributing to fertility decline, postponement of childbearing has other lasting consequences, increasing the probability that women remain childless or have fewer children than desired. It also increases health risks for both mothers and children.

Women are delaying getting married. In general, countries with higher fertility rates in 2005 also display higher share of births outside marriage (GE2.3). However, cross-country variations are very large. For example both the proportions of births outside marriage and fertility rates are low in countries like Japan, Korea and several Southern European countries, where having children is still closely associated to being married.

Further reading

D'Addio, A.C. and M. Mira d'Ercole (2005), "Trends and Determinants of Fertility Rates in OECD Countries: the Role of Policies", OECD Social, Employment and Migration Working Paper, No. 27, OECD, Paris.

OECD (2008), "SF3. Fertility rates", OECD Family database available at: www.oecd.org/els/social/family/database.

Sardon, J. (2006), "Recent Demographic Trends in Europe and the Other Developed Countries", Population, Vol. 61, No. 3, pp. 197-266.

Table and figure notes

Table GE2.2: Note 1: 1992 for Mexico. Note 2: 2001 for New Zealand; 2003 for Mexico. Note 3: 2003 for Finland, Greece, Spain and United Kingdom; 2002 for United States; 2004 for New Zealand; 2006 for Mexico.

Figure GE2.3: Note 1: 2005 for Australia and 2007 for Belgium.

GE2.1. Fertility rates across the OECD are typically below replacement, but a moderate recovery in some countries since the mid-1990s

Total fertility rates from 1970 to 2006

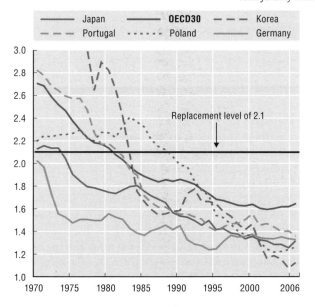

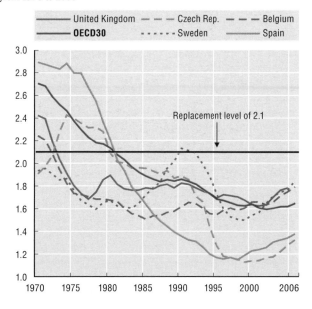

GE2.2. Rising average age of mothers at first childbirth

| | Mean age of mothers at first childbirth | | | |
	1970	1995[1]	2000[2]	2005[3]
Australia	23.2	26.8	..	28.0
Austria	..	25.6	26.4	27.2
Belgium	24.3	27.3	..	27.4
Czech Republic	22.5	23.3	25.0	26.6
Denmark	23.8	27.4	27.7	28.4
Finland	24.4	27.2	27.4	27.9
France	24.4	28.1	27.9	28.5
Germany	24.0	27.5	28.2	28.1
Greece	25.0	26.6	27.5	28.5
Hungary	22.8	23.8	25.1	26.7
Iceland	21.3	25.0	25.5	26.3
Ireland	..	27.3	27.6	28.5
Italy	25.0	28.0	..	28.7
Japan	25.6	27.5	28.0	29.1
Korean	..	..	..	29.1
Luxembourg	24.7	27.4	28.4	29.0
Mexico	..	20.9	21.0	21.3
Netherlands	24.8	28.4	28.6	28.9
New Zealand	..	..	28.0	28.0
Norway	..	26.4	26.9	27.7
Poland	22.8	23.8	24.5	25.8
Portugal	..	25.8	26.5	27.4
Slovak Republic	22.6	23.0	24.2	25.7
Spain	..	28.4	29.1	29.3
Sweden	25.9	27.2	27.9	28.7
Switzerland	25.3	28.1	28.7	29.5
United Kingdom	..	28.3	29.1	29.8
United States	24.1	24.5	24.9	25.1
OECD16	**24.0**	**26.2**	**26.8**	**27.7**

GE2.3. Fertility and births outside marriage are positively related

Share of births outside marriage[1] and total fertility rate, 2006

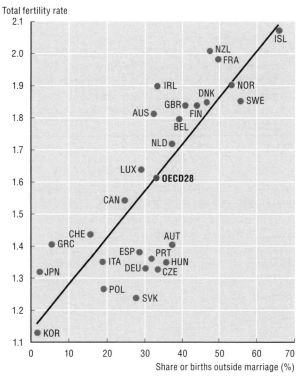

Source: Eurostat and national statistical offices.

StatLink ⟐⟐⟐⟐ http://dx.doi.org/10.1787/550015445534

Definition and measurement

Place of birth and nationality are the two criteria commonly used by OECD countries to define their immigrant population. According to the first criterion, migrants are persons residing in a country but born in another. According to the second criterion, migrants are residents who have a foreign nationality and may include persons born in the host country. Cross-country differences between the size of the foreign-born population and that of the foreign population depend on the rules governing the acquisition of citizenship in each country. In general, the foreign-born population is substantially larger than the foreign population. More information on the origin and characteristics (age, gender, educational level, duration of stay and labour market outcomes) of the immigrant population in OECD countries can be found in the publication *A Profile of Immigrant Populations in the 21th Century*.

Net migration is the number of arrivals of foreigners and of nationals returning from abroad in a given year net of departures of foreigners and nationals in the same year. Although the inflow and outflow data are generally not comparable, the net migration statistics, which are calculated as the difference between inflows and outflows, tend to "net out" the main source of non-comparability in the flow data, namely short-term movements. The OECD annual report *International Migration Outlook* provides a consolidated analysis of recent trends and migration policies in OECD countries.

On average about 12% of the OECD population was foreign-born in 2006. OECD countries differ sharply in the size of their migrant populations. More than half of OECD countries had immigrant populations exceeding 10% of their total population (GE3.1). France (8%) and the United Kingdom (10%) have modest immigrant populations compared to their immediate neighbours Ireland and Spain. The share of the foreign-born was highest in Australia, Canada,

Luxembourg, New Zealand and Switzerland, where it was 20% or more. Mexico and Turkey, countries of high emigration, have negligible foreign-born populations.

OECD foreign-born population shares are growing rapidly. The foreign-born share in the OECD has grown by 2 percentage points since 2000. Some countries, in particular Spain (7%), Ireland (6%) and New Zealand and Austria (both 4%), have registered very high changes in the immigrant share of the population.

On average, net migration contributed up to half of population growth in OECD countries over the last decade. For some countries, net migration accounted for most (*e.g.* Spain) or all (*e.g.* Italy) of the increase in the population over the last ten years (GE3.2). Highest net migration was recorded in Ireland, Luxembourg and Spain.

Gross immigration into the OECD area has increased over the past fifteen years (GE3.3). Net migration flows disguise much larger long term gross flows, both in and out of countries. Many OECD countries are faced with the challenges of economic and social integration of immigrants and their children. At the same time, for some of the non-European OECD countries, emigration of the young, skilled and healthy – the "brain-drain" phenomenon – also constitutes a policy concern.

Further reading

OECD (2007), *Jobs for Immigrants (Vol. 1): Labour Market Integration in Australia, Denmark, Germany and Sweden,* OECD, Paris.

OECD (2008a), *International Migration Outlook,* OECD, Paris.

OECD (2008b), *A Profile of Immigrant Populations in the 21st Century: Data from OECD Countries,* OECD, Paris.

OECD (2008c), *Jobs for Immigrants (Vol. 2): Labour Market Integration in Belgium, France, Netherlands and Portugal,* OECD, Paris.

Figure note

Figure GE3.3: EEA: European Economic Area is the European Union (EU15 for these data) plus Iceland and Norway.

GE3.1. OECD foreign-born populations are growing rapidly

Foreign-born population as a percentage of the total population in 2000 and 2006

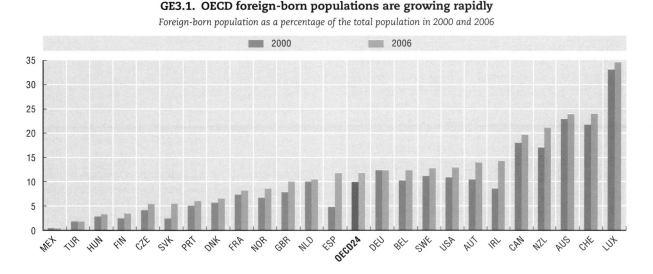

GE3.2. Net migration contributed up to half of population growth in OECD countries over the last decade

Percentage change in population 1996 to 2006 and the contribution of net migration

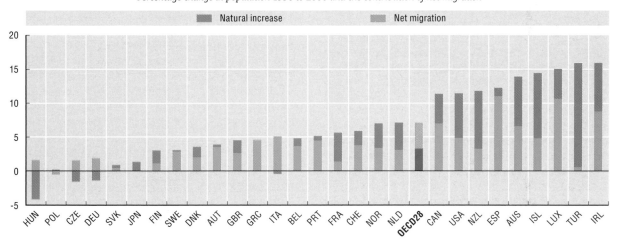

GE3.3. Gross immigration into the OECD area has increased over the last decade

Inflows of foreigners in selected OECD countries, 1990-2006, 1990=100

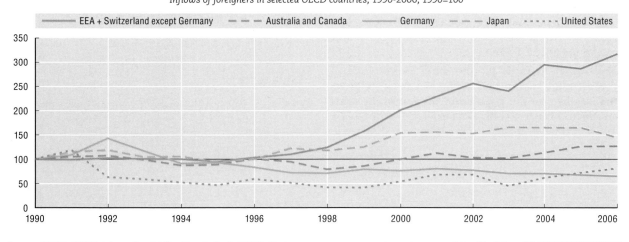

Source: OECD (2008), *International Migration Outlook*, OECD, Paris.   *StatLink* ᔉᘓᔈ http://dx.doi.org/10.1787/550026105721

Definition and measurement

The crude marriage rate is the annual number of new marriages as a population ratio. The crude divorce rate is the annual number of marriages legally ended as a population ratio. Marriage and divorce statistics are based on administrative registers. Marriage rates disregard informal family formation as well as formation of other types of legal unions. Divorce rates miss separation of these unmeasured unions, as well as separation without divorce.

Marriage and divorce rates indicate flows into and out of the state of marriage. Information on the relationship status of the population stock is taken from the *European Social Survey* 2006-07 for 17 OECD countries. Not only does it measure those living together and legally married, it measures the prevalence of civil partnerships which are a new feature on the social landscape in several OECD countries, as well as cohabiting couples. Additionally, the data include same-sex as well as opposite-sex couples cohabiting and in civil partnerships. There may be differences between this survey data and other sources of marital status for individual countries, due to sample variance and non-response bias.

Marriage rates have fallen in most OECD countries. In 2006, the crude marriage rate averaged across 26 OECD countries was 5.1 per 1 000 people, more than a third less than in 1970. The pace of the decline in marriage rates differs across OECD countries. The post-1990 decline was sharp in the Czech Republic, Korea, and the United States while Spain and Sweden show stable or even rising rates since the late 1990s (GE4.1).

Divorce rates have risen in most OECD countries. In 2005, the crude divorce rate was on average 2.3 per 1 000 people, twice the level recorded in 1970 and 0.2 points higher than in 2000. Post-1990, divorce rates fell in the United States but rose in Portugal, Poland, Spain and Japan (GE4.2).

Legal marriage is by far the most common form of adult relationship across the OECD, but significant numbers of the population cohabit or, in some countries, are in a civil partnership (Table GE4.3). More than 60% of the adult population are married in Portugal and Switzerland, but only 44% in Sweden. Civil partnership, even where legally available, is much less popular than marriage, but it exceeds 5% of the adult population in Belgium (in fact there are more Belgians in civil partnership than are cohabiting), the Netherlands and Hungary. High rates of cohabitation are a feature of the Nordic countries, especially Sweden, and of France. Rates of cohabitation are especially low in the Slovak Republic, Hungary and Poland. France has the lowest proportion of singles at 28% and Poland the highest at 42%.

While men are typically older than women when they first get married, the age gap between men and women at the time of first marriage exhibits divergent patterns between countries. The male-female age difference in the age at first marriage has increased in Luxembourg and Austria between 1990 and 2003 (GE4.4). By contrast, the postponement in women's age at first marriage has been accompanied by a large decrease in the male-female age gap in Ireland.

Further reading

Dickmann, A. and K. Schmidheiny (2006), "The Intergenerational Transmission of Divorce – A Fifteen-Country Study with the Fertility and Family Survey", Paper presented at the 2004 Annual Meeting of the Population Association of America.

Morrison, D. and M. Coiro (1999), "Parental Conflict and Marital Disruption: Do Children Benefit When High-Conflict Marriages are Dissolved?", *Journal of Marriage and the Family*, Vol. 61, No. 3, pp. 626-637.

OECD (2008), "SF8. Marriage and divorce rates", *OECD Family Database* available at: *www.oecd.org/els/social/family/database*.

Smock, P. (2004), "The Wax and Wane of Marriage: Prospects for Marriage in the 21st Century", *Journal of Marriage and the Family*, Vol. 66, No. 4, pp. 966-973.

Sobotka T. and L. Toulemon (2008), "Changing Family and Partnership Behaviour: Common Trends and Persistent Diversity across Europe", *Demographic Research*, Vol. 19, No. 6, pp. 85-138.

Table note

Table GE4.3: There was no data for Austria in categories other than married. Missing civil partnership data indicate the lack of this relationship form.

GE4.1. Marriage rates are generally declining

Marriages per 1 000 population, 1970-2006

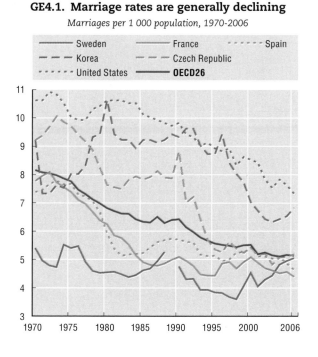

GE4.2. Divorce rates are generally rising

Divorces per 1 000 population, 1970-2006

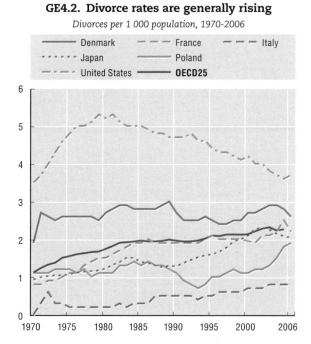

GE4.3. Marriage, civil partnership and cohabitation

Percentages of adult population, 2006-07

	Married	Civil partnership	Cohabitants	Singles	Total
Austria	52	..	..	..	..
Belgium	54	7	6	34	100
Denmark	57	1	13	30	100
Finland	51	0	15	34	100
France	56	2	14	28	100
Germany	54	1	8	36	100
Hungary	53	6	3	37	100
Ireland	55	0	7	37	100
Netherlands	56	6	8	30	100
Norway	50	3	14	33	100
Poland	56	0	2	42	100
Portugal	62	0	4	34	100
Slovak Rep.	56	5	1	39	100
Spain	55	3	4	38	100
Sweden	44	1	21	35	100
Switzerland	61	2	6	31	100
United Kingdom	54	4	6	36	100
OECD	**54**	**3**	**8**	**35**	**100**

GE4.4. Changing male-female age gaps at first marriage

Change from 1990 to 2003 in the difference in mean age at first marriage between men and women

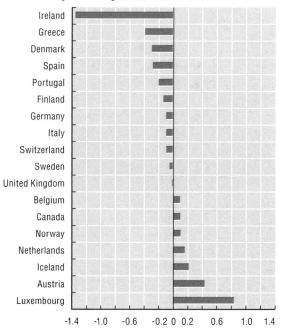

Source: Figures GE4.1, GE4.2, GE4.4 based on Eurostat and national sources; GE4.3 based on European Social Survey 2006-07.

StatLink ⬛ᴹˢ http://dx.doi.org/10.1787/550077543104

5. SELF-SUFFICIENCY INDICATORS

1. Employment

2. Unemployment

3. Childcare

4. Student performance

5. Not in employment, education or training

6. Age of labour force exit

7. Spending on education

Definition and measurement

A person is employed if working for pay, profit or family gain for at least one hour per week, even if temporarily absent from work because of illness, holidays or industrial disputes. The data from labour force surveys of OECD countries rely on this work definition during a survey reference week. The basic indicator for employment is the proportion of the working-age population aged 15-64 who are employed. These employment rates are presented by age, gender, educational attainment and migrant status.

This section also presents data on the incidence of part-time as a percentage of total employment. Part-time employment is defined as people who usually work less than 30 hours per week in their main job. The data include only persons answering questions about their usual hours of work. The OECD data on employment are gathered through national labour force surveys.

Employment rates among the working-age population have increased in most OECD countries since the mid-1990s. In many OECD countries, employment rates in 2007 were higher than during the 1980s (SS1.1). The increase in employment rates since 1995 has exceeded 5 percentage points in Australia, Belgium, Canada, Finland, Greece, Iceland, Italy and the Netherlands, and even 10 points in Ireland and Spain. Conversely, employment rates are 1 to 3 points lower than in the mid-1990s in Czech Republic and Poland, and more than 5 points lower in Turkey. Cross-country differences in employment rates remain substantial. Employment rates exceed 70% or more in fourteen countries including Australia, Canada, Netherlands, Sweden, the United Kingdom and the United States and fall below 60% in Hungary, Italy, Poland and Turkey (Table SS1.3).

The young and the elderly are much less likely to be employed than prime age workers (SS1.2, Table SS1.3). This age pattern is found in all OECD countries, reflecting the fact that many young people are in education, those youth who are active in the labour market have little accumulated job experience and many older people are moving into retirement, even before age 65.

Women are significantly less likely to be employed than men. Employment rates for women are 16 percentage points lower than those of men in 2007. Variability exists, but the basic pattern holds across all countries. In Greece, Italy, Mexico and Turkey, female employment rates are less than 50%, while they exceed 70% in Canada, Denmark, Iceland, Norway, Sweden and Switzerland. Male rates are more similar across countries. Countries where the differences between male and female employment rates are small include Finland and Sweden. Large gaps are found in Turkey and Mexico.

People with low education qualifications are much less likely to have jobs. This pattern is pronounced across the entire OECD and without a single country exception. For this reason OECD governments are extremely focused on education as a means of achieving self-sufficiency.

Migrants are slightly less likely to be employed than the native-born population. However the average OECD employment gap is small compared to the other dimensions examined in SS1.3. Migrants are actually more likely than natives to be in work in Hungary, Italy and Luxembourg (by 7 or more percentage points), but conversely much less likely to be employed in the Netherlands, Denmark and Poland (by 15 or more percentage points).

The recent financial crisis is likely to put downward pressure on employment rates in late 2008 and into 2009. The extent and duration of any decline is as yet unclear.

Figure notes

Figure SS1.2: Data are ranked in ascending order of female employment rates. Data for the low skilled, defined as those with less than an upper secondary education, is for 2006.

Table SS1.3: Note 1: 2006 by educational attainment. Note 2: 2006 for Canada, Iceland and the United States.

SS1.1. More people are in work

Employment to population ratio, persons aged 15 to 64

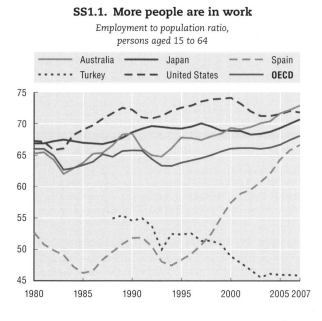

SS1.2. Still large differences in employment rates between socio-demographic groups

Employment rates by group, 2007

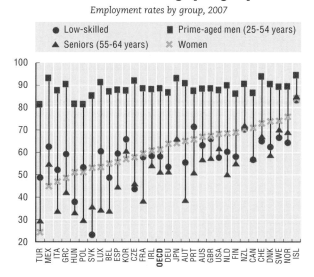

SS1.3 Employment indicators, 2007

| | Employment to population ratio for population aged 15-64 | Employment to population ratio by: | | | | | | | | | | Incidence of part-time employment in percentage of employment | | |
| | | Age | | | Gender | | Educational level[1] | | | Immigrant status[2] | | | | |
		15-24	25-54	55-64	Men	Women	Less than upper secondary education	Upper secondary education	Tertiary education	Native-born	Foreign-born	Total	Men	Women
Australia	72.9	64.2	80.0	56.7	79.6	66.1	63.5	80.4	84.4	74.9	67.5	24.1	12.4	38.5
Austria	71.4	55.5	84.0	38.6	78.4	64.4	55.7	75.8	85.9	72.7	65.0	17.2	5.2	31.5
Belgium	61.6	26.8	79.3	33.8	68.2	54.9	49.0	73.2	83.6	63.5	50.9	18.3	6.3	32.9
Canada	73.6	59.5	82.2	57.1	77.2	70.1	57.0	76.0	82.8	73.0	70.5	18.2	11.0	26.1
Czech Republic	66.1	28.5	83.5	46.0	74.8	57.3	43.9	75.6	85.1	66.1	67.3	3.5	1.7	5.9
Denmark	77.3	67.4	86.1	58.7	81.3	73.3	62.8	81.3	87.4	78.8	62.7	17.7	12.4	23.9
Finland	70.5	46.4	83.3	55.0	72.4	68.5	58.4	75.6	85.0	70.5	63.5	11.7	8.2	15.5
France	64.0	30.1	82.1	38.3	68.6	59.4	58.1	75.6	83.0	65.3	58.5	13.4	5.0	23.1
Germany	69.0	45.9	80.3	51.3	74.7	63.2	53.8	72.5	84.3	70.9	61.1	22.2	7.9	39.2
Greece	61.5	24.2	75.7	42.1	74.9	48.1	59.5	69.7	83.3	60.9	66.6	7.8	4.1	13.6
Hungary	57.3	21.0	74.6	33.1	64.0	50.9	38.2	70.4	81.8	57.2	64.6	2.8	1.6	4.2
Iceland	85.7	74.3	89.4	84.9	89.5	81.7	83.6	88.6	92.0	84.6	84.2	15.9	8.0	25.4
Ireland	69.0	48.8	78.8	54.1	77.4	60.3	58.7	77.3	86.5	68.2	72.9	20.3	7.6	35.6
Italy	58.7	24.7	73.5	33.8	70.7	46.6	52.5	74.4	80.6	58.0	65.9	15.1	5.4	29.9
Japan	70.7	41.5	80.2	66.1	81.7	59.5		73.1	79.8	..	..	18.9	9.2	32.6
Korea	63.9	25.7	74.0	60.6	74.7	53.2	66.2	70.3	77.2	..	..	8.9	6.3	12.5
Luxembourg	63.0	22.1	80.1	34.3	72.4	53.5	60.8	73.4	85.2	59.2	71.1	13.1	1.6	28.8
Mexico	61.1	44.2	70.3	54.7	80.9	43.6	62.8	73.1	83.3	..	..	15.1	8.1	27.6
Netherlands	74.1	65.4	83.6	50.1	80.0	68.1	60.6	79.1	86.4	77.0	62.4	36.1	16.2	60.0
New Zealand	75.4	58.7	82.2	72.0	82.1	69.0	70.6	84.5	84.6	..	..	22.0	11.2	34.7
Norway	77.5	56.0	85.8	69.0	80.4	74.6	64.7	83.1	89.2	77.2	69.9	20.4	10.5	31.6
Poland	57.0	25.8	74.9	29.7	63.6	50.6	53.6	65.6	83.5	57.1	36.8	10.1	6.0	15.0
Portugal	67.8	34.9	81.0	50.9	73.9	61.9	71.7	80.2	86.4	67.3	73.1	10.0	6.3	14.3
Slovak Republic	60.7	27.6	78.0	35.7	68.4	53.0	23.5	71.9	84.9	60.7	66.0	2.6	1.2	4.4
Spain	66.6	42.9	76.8	44.6	77.4	55.5	59.8	75.9	83.4	64.4	70.3	10.9	3.8	20.9
Sweden	75.7	46.3	86.1	70.1	78.0	73.2	66.9	81.9	87.3	76.2	63.1	14.4	9.5	19.7
Switzerland	78.6	62.6	86.1	67.2	85.6	71.6	65.3	80.1	90.2	80.3	73.7	25.4	8.7	45.6
Turkey	45.8	30.4	54.2	29.4	67.9	23.8	49.0	62.7	75.5	45.7	48.7	8.4	4.6	19.2
United Kingdom	72.3	55.9	81.3	57.4	78.4	66.3	66.3	80.7	88.1	71.8	66.3	23.3	9.9	38.6
United States	71.8	53.1	79.9	61.8	77.8	65.9	58.0	73.3	82.7	69.5	70.8	12.6	7.6	17.9
OECD	**68.0**	**43.7**	**79.6**	**51.2**	**75.8**	**60.3**	**58.4**	**75.9**	**84.4**	**68.1**	**65.1**	**15.3**	**7.2**	**25.6**

Source: OECD (2008), *OECD Employment Outlook*, OECD, Paris (www.oecd.org/els/employment/outlook); and OECD (2008), *International Migration Outlook* (www.oecd.org/els/migration/imo).

StatLink 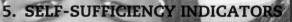 http://dx.doi.org/10.1787/550148582371

Definition and measurement

The unemployment rate is the ratio of people out of work and actively seeking it to the population of working age either in work or actively seeking it (15 to 64-years old). The data are gathered through labour force surveys of member countries. According to the standardised ILO definition used in these surveys, the unemployed are those who did not work for at least one hour in the reference week of the survey but who are currently available for work and who have taken specific steps to seek employment in the four weeks preceding the survey. Thus, for example, people who cannot work because of physical impairment, or who are not actively seeking a job because they have little hope of finding work are not considered as unemployed.

This section also presents data on the incidence of long-term unemployment among all unemployed persons. Long-term unemployment is defined in two alternative ways: those who have been unemployed more than six months and those unemployed for more than 12 months.

In 2007 the average OECD unemployment rate was 5.7%. Unemployment rates were under 3% in Iceland and Norway. Unemployment rates remain above 10% in the Slovak Republic and Turkey (Table SS2.3).

The average OECD unemployment rate fell about one percentage point between 2005 and 2007. Unemployment had previously moderately increased for four consecutive years since 2001 (SS2.1). However, developments have been quite diverse across countries over the same period. Declines occurred in 15 countries (notably in the Slovak Republic, Spain and Poland) and increases occurred in another 15 (including Germany, Portugal and Sweden). The recent financial crisis is also likely to push unemployment rates up across many OECD countries.

Young people, migrants and less educated people are more likely to be unemployed. The age pattern holds for all 30 countries. The average unemployment rate of young people across OECD countries (12%) is much higher than that of both working age 25-54 (5%) and older people (4%). The unemployment rate of immigrants is somewhat elevated compared to the native-born (on average 3 percentage points higher). This pattern does not hold in Hungary, Turkey, or the United States, where immigrant unemployment is lower. However, in Switzerland, Austria, Belgium, the Netherlands and Nordic countries, the unemployment rate of immigrants is more than double that of the native-born population. The education pattern holds for all countries except in Mexico, Korea and Turkey, where more educated people are slightly more likely to be unemployed.

There has been some welcome convergence of female and male unemployment rates across many countries. Currently, women are on average only marginally more likely to be unemployed than men. However the four Mediterranean countries – Greece, Spain, Italy and Portugal – still have unemployment gaps to the detriment of women in 2007 at or over 3 percentage points. SS2.2 shows that at the beginning of the 1990s the gender gap was actually considerably higher in three out of four of these countries than in 2007. Greece is the exception with little reduction in gender inequality.

Figure and table notes

Figure SS2.2: The closest figures to 1990 were 1991 for Iceland, Mexico and Switzerland, 1992 for Hungary and Poland, 1993 for the Czech Republic, 1994 for Austria and the Slovak Republic.

Table SS2.3: Note 1: 2006 by educational attainment. Note 2: 2006 for Canada, Iceland and the United States.

SOCIETY AT A GLANCE 2009: OECD SOCIAL INDICATORS – ISBN 978-92-64-04938-3 – © OECD 2009

SS2.1. The OECD unemployment rate is in decline

Unemployment rate, age 15-64, percentage of the labour force, 1980-2007

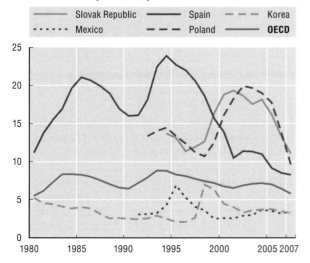

SS2.2. Gender gaps in unemployment to the detriment of women are generally declining

Percentage point differences in unemployment rates between females and males 1990 or closest year and 2007

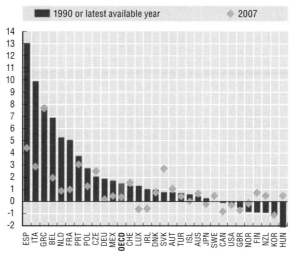

SS2.3. Unemployment indicators, 2007

| | Unemployment rate for the population aged 15-64 | Unemployment rate by: | | | | | | | | | | Incidence of long-term unemployment in percentage of unemployment | |
| | | Age | | | Gender | | Educational level[1] | | | Immigrant status[2] | | | |
		15-24	25-54	55-64	Men	Women	Less than upper secondary education	Upper secondary education	Tertiary education	Native-born	Foreign-born	6 months and over	12 months and over
Australia	4.4	9.4	3.4	2.7	4.1	4.8	6.2	3.9	2.8	4.1	4.7	27.1	15.5
Austria	4.5	8.7	3.8	3.0	4.0	5.1	7.8	3.8	2.9	3.5	9.0	44.2	26.8
Belgium	7.7	19.2	6.8	3.8	6.7	8.8	11.7	6.9	3.9	6.4	16.4	68.1	50.0
Canada	6.1	11.2	5.1	5.0	6.4	5.7	9.9	6.1	4.7	6.5	7.0	14.8	7.5
Czech Republic	5.4	10.7	4.9	4.6	4.3	6.8	23.0	6.4	2.0	5.3	9.0	71.6	53.4
Denmark	3.6	7.2	2.7	4.2	3.3	4.1	7.8	4.8	3.9	3.4	8.2	29.5	18.2
Finland	6.9	15.7	5.3	6.5	6.5	7.3	12.0	8.2	4.7	6.7	14.4	37.9	23.0
France	8.0	18.7	6.9	5.1	7.5	8.6	12.1	7.6	6.2	7.4	13.4	58.5	40.4
Germany	8.7	11.7	8.0	10.3	8.6	8.9	20.5	11.2	5.5	7.8	14.3	71.3	56.6
Greece	8.2	22.0	7.6	3.4	5.0	12.8	8.4	9.7	6.9	8.4	8.7	68.2	50.3
Hungary	7.4	18.0	6.8	4.2	7.2	7.7	10.8	5.0	1.9	7.5	4.3	64.0	47.5
Iceland	2.3	7.2	1.3	0.9	2.3	2.4	3.1	2.8	1.0	2.9	..	11.1	8.0
Ireland	4.6	8.7	4.1	2.6	4.9	4.3	6.4	3.2	2.1	4.4	5.9	50.1	30.3
Italy	6.2	20.3	5.3	2.4	5.0	7.9	7.8	5.3	4.8	6.0	7.9	65.4	49.9
Japan	4.1	7.7	3.7	3.4	4.1	3.9	6.7	5.4	3.7	..	..	47.5	32.0
Korea	3.4	8.8	3.1	2.2	3.8	2.8	2.6	3.5	2.9	..	..	11.7	0.6
Luxembourg	3.9	14.9	3.3	0.7	4.1	3.5	5.0	3.8	3.0	3.6	4.6	54.7	33.5
Mexico	3.5	6.7	2.7	1.6	3.3	3.8	1.9	2.8	3.0	..	..	5.4	2.7
Netherlands	3.7	7.3	2.7	4.1	3.2	4.2	5.7	3.9	2.8	3.1	7.6	59.1	41.7
New Zealand	3.7	9.7	2.5	1.4	3.4	3.9	4.2	2.4	2.4	4.8	6.0	16.7	5.7
Norway	2.5	7.5	1.9	1.0	2.6	2.5	3.6	3.8	2.4	2.3	5.1	25.1	8.5
Poland	9.7	21.7	8.4	6.8	9.1	10.4	27.8	17.4	6.2	9.7	9.5	64.3	45.9
Portugal	8.5	16.6	7.8	6.5	7.0	10.1	6.4	5.6	4.4	8.4	9.6	67.6	47.3
Slovak Republic	11.0	20.1	10.1	8.1	9.8	12.6	47.7	14.6	4.8	11.2	..	82.3	70.8
Spain	8.3	18.2	7.2	5.9	6.4	10.9	11.0	9.5	7.3	7.9	10.3	42.6	27.6
Sweden	6.2	18.9	4.4	3.9	5.9	6.4	6.5	5.8	4.3	5.3	12.1	27.3	13.0
Switzerland	3.7	7.1	3.1	3.1	3.0	4.6	7.2	3.7	2.8	2.6	7.1	56.6	40.8
Turkey	10.1	19.6	8.3	3.8	10.0	10.5	8.1	10.1	8.2	8.7	8.3	46.3	30.4
United Kingdom	5.3	14.4	3.7	3.3	5.6	4.9	6.6	3.7	2.2	4.9	7.6	41.5	24.7
United States	4.7	10.5	3.7	3.1	4.8	4.6	10.5	5.6	3.3	5.3	4.4	17.6	10.0
OECD	**5.7**	**11.9**	**4.9**	**4.0**	**5.5**	**6.0**	**10.3**	**6.2**	**3.9**	**5.7**	**8.6**	**42.3**	**29.1**

Source: OECD (2008), Employment Outlook (www.oecd.org/els/employment/outlook) and OECD (2008), International Migration Outlook (www.oecd.org/els/migration/imo).

StatLink ᵃᵐˢ⁄ http://dx.doi.org/10.1787/550176642218

Definitions and measurement

Childcare enrolment among 0-2 year-olds includes enrolment in formal arrangements such as childcare centres, registered child minders, as well as care provided by someone who is not a family member. Enrolment rates for 3-5-year-olds refer to those enrolled in formal pre-school services, and in some countries for 4- and 5-year-olds in primary schools.

Data on childcare participation of the 0-2 year-olds comes from various sources, limiting comparability, including *OECD Babies and Bosses reviews*, the *OECD Education database*, the Eurydice database, NOSOSCO reviews and National Statistical Offices. Enrolment for 3-5-year-olds is presented using data of the *OECD Education database*. This information is based upon actual numbers of students participating in formal pre-school programmes and a percentage is calculated by using population data as a denominator.

On average across the OECD one in five children under the age of three is enrolled in formal childcare (SS3.1). While enrolment rates of very young children are less than 10% in Austria, the Czech Republic, Germany, Greece, Hungary, Italy, Mexico and Poland, around 40% or more of children in this age group use childcare facilities in the Nordic countries. Participation rates are especially high in Denmark (62%) and Iceland (59%). This country variation reflects variation in public provision of childcare, in parental leave systems, in other incentives for women to work, and in culture and family structures. The enrolment figures do not reflect time in care. The amount of hours young children spend in formal care probably also varies considerably across countries. These differences may be important because intensity of childcare plays an important role in both children's developmental outcomes (hours can be either too much or too little) and in maternal labour market engagement.

Cross-country comparisons are, however, fraught because of data issues. It is possible that formal childcare is under-reported in countries where a significant proportion of childcare is provided privately in centres or by non-family carers in the home (*e.g.* Australia, Canada, Ireland, Mexico and the United States) or in countries where early childhood education and care is delivered and financed by local government (*e.g.* Canada, Mexico, Switzerland and the United States). This under-reporting may lead to an underestimation of enrolment rates. Additionally, in some countries young children may be enrolled in several part-time programmes, leading to double counting issues, and consequently to an overestimation of enrolment rates.

On average across the OECD more than 70% of children aged 3-5 are enrolled in pre-school (SS3.2). The proportion is much higher than childcare participation for younger children. In half of OECD countries, at least 80% of children in this age group were enrolled in pre-school programmes in 2006. Enrolment rates are practically universal in France, Belgium, Italy and Spain. On the other hand, few in Turkey, Poland and Korea participate, reflecting considerable reliance on family care.

More children attend pre-school than in the past. Between 2000 and 2005, average pre-school enrolment rates of children aged 3-5 years increased by 4 percentage points, from 69% to 73%. Countries with large rises include Germany, Mexico and Norway.

The Nordic countries, France and Belgium spend the highest proportion of their net national income on childcare (SS3.3). At the lower end are Switzerland, Korea, Canada and Greece. The variation observed in spending across countries reflects differences in population shares of young children, in enrolment rates, and in spending per child between countries.

Further reading

OECD (various issues), *Babies and Bosses*, OECD, Paris. (*www.oecd.org/els/social/family*).

OECD (2008), *Education at a Glance*, OECD, Paris.

Figure note

Figure SS3.1: Countries are ranked in descending order of 3- to 5-year old enrolment rates. No data for Switzerland and Turkey; 2000 for Ireland and Italy; 2001 for Germany and Poland; 2002 for France; 2003 for Greece, Iceland, Luxembourg, Mexico, Norway and the Slovak Republic; 2005 for Australia, Denmark, Korea and the United States; 2004 for other countries.

SS3.1. Enrolment in formal childcare varies widely across countries

Average enrolment rate of children aged under 3 in formal childcare, 2005 or latest year available, percentage

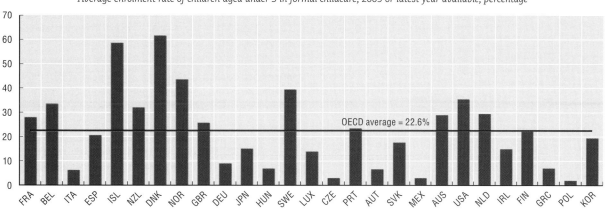

OECD average = 22.6%

SS3.2. A majority of pre-school children aged 3-5 are in childcare

Average enrolment rate of children aged 3- to 5-years of age in pre-school educational programmes, percentage, 2000 and 2005

■ 2006 values ◆ 2000 values —— 2006 average (73%) – – – 2000 average (69%)

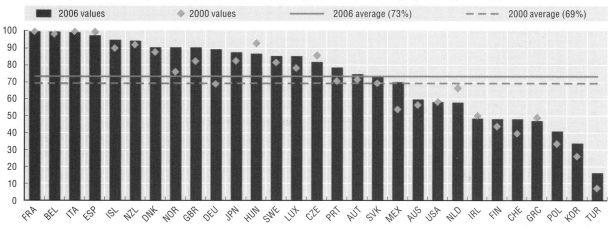

SS3.3. Nordic countries spend significantly more on childcare programmes

Public spending on childcare including pre-primary education, percentage of NNI, 2005

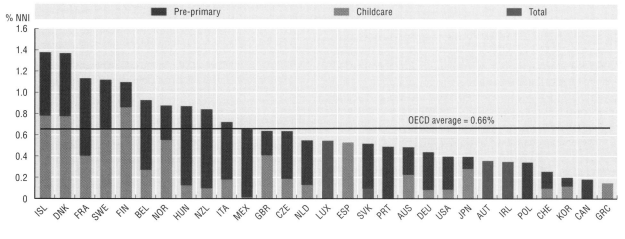

■ Pre-primary ▨ Childcare ■ Total

OECD average = 0.66%

Source: OECD Family database (www.oecd.org/els/social/family/database).

StatLink ⬛⬛ http://dx.doi.org/10.1787/550177446630

Definition and measurement

Student performance can be assessed through results from the OECD Programme for International Student Assessment (PISA). PISA is the most comprehensive international effort to measure the skills of students towards the end of the period of compulsory education. In the latest results, 15-year-old students across the OECD did tests in reading, mathematics and science in 2006 (the United States is not included in the reading test). In PISA comparable tests are administered under independently supervised conditions in order to assess students' competencies. PISA tests are not tied to specific national curricula. Rather, students apply knowledge to situations they might encounter in the real word, such as planning a route, interpreting the instructions for an electrical appliance, or taking information from a figure. For each subject the average score across OECD countries is 500 for the first time it becomes a major domain in PISA. Thereafter the OECD average reflects the performance of the OECD countries.

PISA results from the 2006 wave in reading can be compared to those from the 2000 wave, which gives the longest period for consideration of time trends (science and maths results are, unfortunately, not comparable over this longer time period).

In addition to the mean test scores for students in each country in the three subjects, a measure of inequality in test scores within countries, the coefficient of variation (defined as the country standard deviation divided by the average score), is also used.

Poor student performance at age 15 can have lasting life cycle implications for young people. Poor learning outcomes lead to a higher probability of dropping out of school, worse longer term career and relationship prospects, and greater probability of long term welfare dependence. Thus ensuring that children get a good education is a policy priority in all OECD countries. All countries spend large but varying amounts of public money to ensure that youngsters are educated. Student performance in the PISA tests indicates the cumulative effect of educational inputs from family,

schools, peers and the community up to age 15. While test score performance is not the only indicator of successful schooling (socialisation is clearly an important goal, for example), it is almost universally regarded as a highly important measure.

Cross-country differences in the performance of students towards the end of compulsory schooling are large (SS4.1). Differences between the top country (Korea for reading, Finland for maths and science) and the bottom country (Mexico) exceed 140 points, which is nearly one and a half standard deviations. SS4.1 also illustrates a strong tendency for countries which do well in reading to also do well in maths and science. Country correlations between reading, mathematics and science scores are all in excess of 0.87.

The reading gender gap in favour of girls has been rising over time. Gender gaps in reading scores are increasing across almost all the OECD countries over the period 2000-06 (SS4.2). While in the majority of country cases this rise is not statistically significant, the fact that the trend is found in all but two countries suggests systematic changes may be occurring in favour of girls. The 2006 results also confirm, contrary to the reading result, boys do better than girls in maths. Science is a mixed bag. Unfortunately the maths and science gender gaps cannot be compared over the same period.

Countries where average reading test scores have *grown* between 2000 and 2006 have also seen *reductions* in their test score inequality (SS4.3). The correlation between the change in reading scores and the change in reading score inequality (measured by the coefficient of variation of reading scores), is –0.52. Previous editions of *Society at a Glance* had shown that countries with high average PISA scores levels also have low test score level inequality and *vice versa*.

Further reading

OECD (2003), *Literacy Skills for the World of Tomorrow: Further Results from PISA 2000*, OECD, Paris.

OECD (2007), *PISA 2006: Science Competencies for Tomorrow's World*, OECD, Paris (*www.pisa.oecd.org*).

Figure notes

Figure SS4.1: PISA: OECD Programme for International Student Assessment. Countries are ranked, from top to bottom in decreasing order of student performance in mathematics.

SS4.1. Large differences in students' performance among OECD countries

Mean scores on the mathematics, reading and science scales, PISA 2006

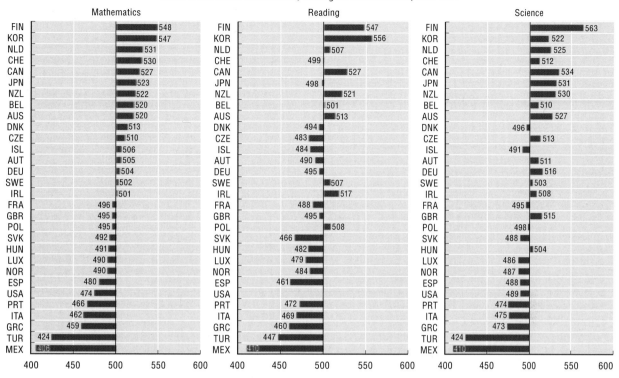

SS4.2. Gender gaps in favour of girls in reading are rising

Changes in gender differences in reading (female less male scores) between 2000 and 2006, points

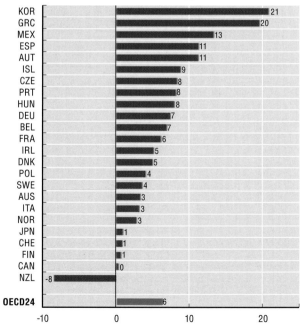

SS4.3. Countries with rising average reading test scores have reductions in test score inequality

Changes in average reading scores and changes in the coefficient of variation of reading scores

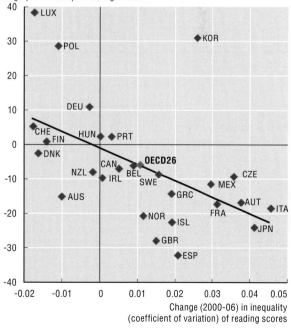

Source: OECD (2007), *PISA 2006: Science Competencies for Tomorrow's World*, OECD, Paris (www.pisa.oecd.org).

StatLink ⟡ http://dx.doi.org/10.1787/550180640382

Definition and measurement

This indicator records those aged 15-19 not in education and not in employment or training as a proportion of the age group population. The only exception to the 15-19-year-old age band is Japan, where the indicator covers youth population aged 15 to 24 years. Education includes both part-time and full-time education, but not non-formal and very short duration education. Data are gathered through labour force surveys and typically refer to the four week preceding the survey. Data may be volatile over time due to sampling error. Rates are reported for the years 1998 to 2006. Data are taken from OECD *Education at a Glance 2008*.

Youth not in employment, education or training are in a minority. About 6% of youth were, on average, not in employment, education or training across the OECD in 2006. The average conceals considerable country variation. Rates are nearly twice this average in Italy, New Zealand, Spain, and the United Kingdom. Conversely, not in employment, education or training rates are roughly half the average OECD rate in Norway and Poland.

Proportions not in employment, education or training are declining across OECD countries. Not in employment, education or training rates for males fell from around 8% in 1998 to a little above 6% in 2006, and for females the decline was similar. However, the vast majority of the decline took place between 1998 and 2002. Thereafter average OECD rates have been fairly stable. Main drivers behind the decline include falls in the Slovak Republic (a reduction of 15 percentage points for boys and 8 percentage points for girls between 1998 and 2000), and Hungary (6 percentage points less for both boys and girls). Countries where not in employment, education or training rates have bucked the OECD trend and risen over the period for both boys and girls include Denmark, France, Japan, Switzerland and the United Kingdom.

Not in employment, education or training rates are converging across the OECD. Male rates are less dispersed across the OECD than female rates.

The majority of youth not in employment, education or training are not seeking work (SS5.3). Only in the Slovak and Czech Republics, France, Poland and Austria are more than half of these young people actively seeking work. At the other end of the spectrum, Mexico and Turkey have fewer than 15% of youth not in employment, education or training ready and willing to work.

Males not in employment, education or training are more likely to be seeking work than inactive females. In only three countries – Poland, Austria and Denmark – are there more young female than male jobseekers. One explanation for females being less likely to seek work is that they are more likely to be involved in looking after a child. Poland, Austria, and Denmark, where young females are more likely to be seeking work, are all countries with relatively low rates of teen births. Where the male-female gap in terms of seeking work is greatest, as in Mexico and Turkey, teen birth rates are correspondingly high.

Figure and table notes

Tables SS5.1 and SS5.2: Only countries with up-to-date results for 2006 have been included in the comparisons. Japanese data is for youth aged 15 to 24. Iceland, Mexico and Turkey are missing.

Figure SS5.3: Japanese data is for youth aged 15 to 24. Iceland, Luxembourg and Norway are missing. Inactive youth available for work refers to those who are actively seeking, or can take up, employment. Figures for males in the Slovak Republic, and females in Finland, Sweden and Greece are estimates based on reported figures for females in the Slovak Republic, and males in Finland, Sweden and Greece, and reported totals.

SS5.1. Young males not in employment, education or training in the OECD is relatively stable

Percentage of young males in education and not in education, 1998-2006

	1998	2000	2002	2004	2006
Australia	9.0	6.4	6.9	7.6	6.7
Austria	..	..	8.1	7.2	7.1
Belgium	10.8	6.7	7.3	5.8	7.5
Canada	9.1	8.7	8.7	9.8	8.0
Czech Republic	6.7	7.3	5.8	5.0	4.7
Denmark	..	1.9	2.4	1.9	4.8
Finland	..	..	..	5.4	4.1
France	3.5	3.4	3.7	5.7	6.7
Germany	..	5.2	4.3	3.5	4.1
Greece	6.9	6.9	5.2	8.7	7.9
Hungary	12.4	8.6	8.3	6.6	6.4
Ireland	..	4.5	5.2	5.2	5.3
Italy	14.5	12.2	10.8	11.1	12.2
Japan	5.5	7.3	8.3	8.1	7.5
Luxembourg	6.4	..	..	..	4.4
Netherlands	2.6	3.8	4.0	3.5	3.3
New Zealand	..	..	..	..	9.9
Norway	..	..	..	..	3.5
Poland	4.7	5.0	3.5	3.0	3.8
Portugal	6.9	6.2	7.7	9.0	7.8
Slovak Republic	21.7	27.8	17.7	8.6	6.5
Spain	10.1	7.7	6.9	7.3	9.6
Sweden	6.4	4.7	5.9	6.4	6.2
Switzerland	4.0	7.3	5.8	7.6	7.7
United Kingdom	..	8.2	8.2	9.0	11.5
United States	6.5	6.8	6.4	6.5	6.0

SS5.2. Variation in females not in employment, education or training is greater than for males across the OECD

Percentage of young females in education and not in education, 1998-2006

	1998	2000	2002	2004	2006
Australia	8.7	7.3	7.2	7.4	7.4
Austria	..	..	4.4	7.5	6.0
Belgium	10.8	6.3	6.4	3.9	6.7
Canada	7.9	7.7	7.2	7.6	6.7
Czech Republic	7.7	8.5	6.3	6.4	4.3
Denmark	2.1	3.6	2.4	2.3	4.1
Finland	..	..	..	6.4	3.0
France	2.6	3.2	3.2	4.5	6.2
Germany	..	6.3	5.1	3.7	4.3
Greece	12.7	11.2	7.5	11.3	9.8
Hungary	11.1	8.6	7.8	5.8	5.6
Ireland	..	4.3	4.5	4.6	4.7
Italy	15.9	14.1	10.3	10.9	11.4
Japan	9.8	10.3	10.6	10.4	10.5
Netherlands	2.9	3.6	3.7	3.4	2.6
New Zealand	..	..	..	..	12.7
Norway	..	..	..	..	3.4
Poland	4.9	4.0	2.6	2.1	3.7
Portugal	9.7	9.2	6.8	10.6	7.7
Slovak Republic	14.9	24.7	13.5	7.1	6.8
Spain	9.6	8.2	7.5	7.9	10.6
Sweden	2.9	2.4	3.3	3.2	4.3
Switzerland	5.7	8.5	5.8	6.8	7.5
United Kingdom	..	7.9	8.9	9.0	10.3
United States	8.2	7.3	7.5	7.3	6.7

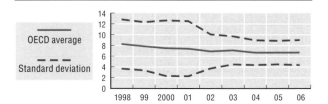

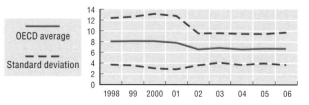

SS5.3. The majority of young females not in employment, education or training are typically unavailable for work

Percentage available for or seeking work by gender, 2006

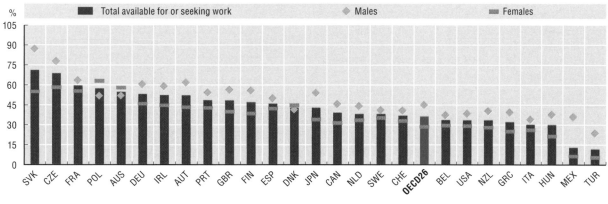

Source: OECD (2008), *Education at a Glance*, OECD, Paris (*www.oecd.org/edu/EAG2008*).

StatLink http://dx.doi.org/10.1787/550204735041

Definition and measurement

Retirement is associated with cessation of work and receipt of a pension. Actual retirement ages are difficult to measure directly without internationally comparable longitudinal data, so international comparisons must rely on indirect measures from cross-sectional data. Indirect measures regard persons above a specified age as "retired" if they are not in the labour force at the time of the survey (average age at labour force exit). Net movements into retirement are proxied by the changes over time in the proportion of the older population not in the labour force. This indirect measure is used in ongoing OECD reviews of older workers. It measures the average effective age of retirement. The official age of retirement is also complex to pin down, especially when retirement is based on fixed years of pension contribution. For more discussion, see OECD (2007).

For both men and women the most common official age of pension entitlement in OECD countries is 65. Higher and lower official ages exist in some countries (see Figure SS6.1). Despite longer female life expectancy and higher average male contribution rates, the average OECD official retirement age is lower for women (62.7 years) than for men (63.6 years).

The decision to retire depends on more than the official retirement age. Relevant factors include physical health, labour market conditions, generosity and tax treatment of retirement income, private savings, family obligations, spousal labour supply, and attitudes in workplaces to older people.

The average effective retirement age is below the official retirement age (SS6.1). There are exceptions. In Japan, Korea and Mexico, the average age exceeds the official age by more than five years. Mexican women work ten years more than the official age and Mexican men eight years more. Korean men also work more than ten years beyond the official age. Similarly, in Turkey, and Greece women and men work several years more that the official age.

The average effective retirement age varies more than official retirement ages between countries. Effective retirement ages are highest in Mexico and Korea, around or in excess of age 70. They are lowest in Hungary, Belgium, the Slovak Republic, Luxembourg, Austria and France, where people withdraw from the labour force and move into retirement when in their late 50s.

Effective retirement ages are rising in many countries, especially for women (SS6.2). Effective retirement ages had fallen significantly over the last 30 years in most OECD countries, excepting in Japan and Korea. This trend has halted or reversed, in response to rising life expectancy, strong labour market conditions and stronger financial incentives for older people to work. Policy changes increasing the official retirement age may have played a role in some countries. Between 1999-2002 and 2002-07 the effective retirement age has risen by more than a year for women in 13 OECD countries and for men in seven OECD countries. Countries with big rises in effective retirement ages for women include Mexico, New Zealand and Turkey. For men large rises were experienced in Korea, New Zealand and Sweden. There are, however, countries where life expectancy is rising and effective retirement ages are in decline (e.g. Iceland for women and Denmark for men). Potentially this pattern can lead to fiscal sustainability problems.

There is little relationship between the actual age at labour force exit and people's life expectancy at a country level. Even the relationship between the legal retirement age – a major policy instrument – and the actual retirement age is far from strong across countries (the correlation is only 0.35).

Further reading

OECD (2007), *Pensions at a Glance*, OECD, Paris.

Figure notes

Figures SS6.1 and SS6.2: The average effective age of retirement is derived from observed changes in participation rates over a five-year period for successive cohorts of workers (by five-year age groups) aged 40 and over. Life expectancy refers to 2005 and change from 2000 to 2005.

SS6.1. Labour force exit rates are generally lower than official retirement ages

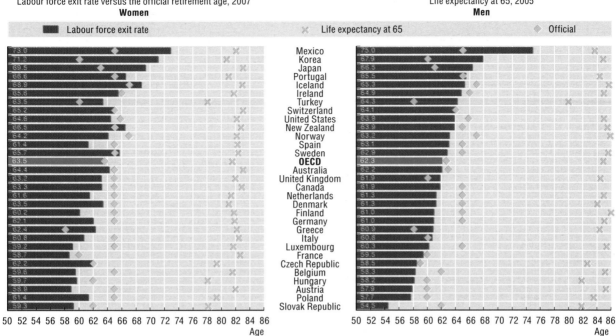

SS6.2. Rising life expectancy compared with changes in official retirement age and in age at labour force exit

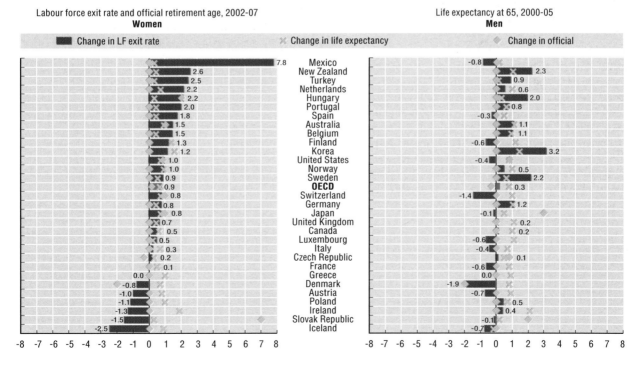

Source: OECD estimates derived from the European and national labour force surveys.

StatLink http://dx.doi.org/10.1787/550222773834

Definition and measurement

Spending on education as a proportion of net national income (NNI) gives a measure of how much money is invested in human capital (it excludes consideration parental time inputs or on-the-job learning or training) relative to the total flow of monetary resources available to society. The indicator measures both public and private expenditure on educational institutions (including public subsidies) and family spending in so far as it translates into payments to educational institutions. Spending data does not include subsidies for student living costs, student loan subsidies and other direct private spending (for example on text books or transport to school). Nor do they measure spending on pre-school education or childcare, which may have an educational component.

Cross country comparisons of educational spending per student are based on purchasing power parity exchange rates and Net National Income measures (see "Definitions and measurement" for GE1. Net national income). It should be noted that use of NNI rather than GDP as a denominator increases education spending shares and changes some country rankings in comparison to the analysis in *OECD Education at a Glance 2008*.

OECD countries spend on average 7% of their net national income on education (SS7.1). Of this 7%, about 1 percentage point is private spending. The proportional total amount spent is variable, exceeding 8% in Iceland, Denmark, New Zealand, Korea and the United States, and falling under 5.5% in Italy, Spain and Greece. Education spending is influenced by the number of children and all three low spending countries have low fertility rates by OECD standards. Of additional interest is the observation that private education spending is smallest in Finland and largest in Korea. Yet both are the top PISA achievers, combining their total spending very effectively but in two quite different ways.

The total amount of education spending has been rising moderately as a percentage of NNI across the OECD over the period 1995-2005 (SS7.2). Large rises took place in particular in Iceland (about 2 percentage points of NNI), the United Kingdom and Mexico (both about 1 percentage point). However, falls were also observed in ten countries over the same period, including Canada, Finland and Norway.

There is a positive relationship between cumulative education spending between the ages of 6 and 15 and country PISA maths scores (SS7.3). However, while solid, the relationship is moderate in strength (the correlation is 0.47). The biggest over-performers, based on their net national income, are the two PISA top performers, Korea and Finland. The Netherlands and New Zealand are also over-performers. Under-performers in education, given their level of National Income, include Turkey, Mexico, Italy and the United States. While education expenditure on the under-age-6 population is not included in Figure SS7.2, such spending tends to be high in the Nordic countries which, with the exception of Finland, do not perform better than predicted. In addition, such early education spending is also very low in Korea, a stand-out PISA performer. It is unlikely that the omission of early education spending is a major reason for the moderate correlation.

Further reading

OECD (2008), *Education at a Glance*, OECD, Paris.

Figure note

Figure SS7.3: PISA: OECD Programme for International Student Assessment.

SS7.1. Total education spending as a share of net national income

In percentage, 2005

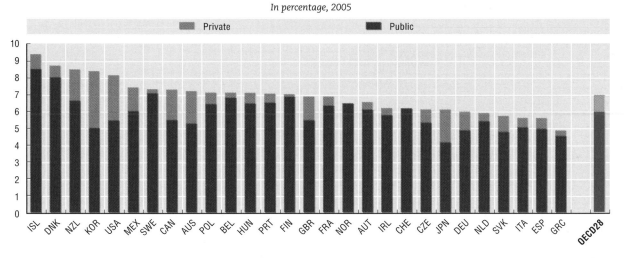

SS7.2. Total education spending as a share of net national income, 1995-2005

In percentage, 1995, 2000, 2005

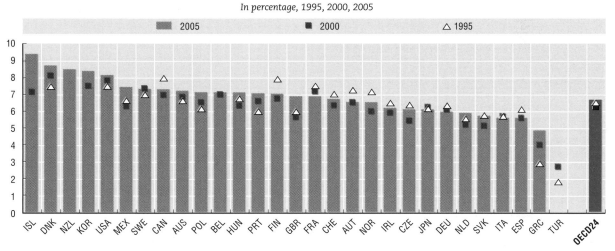

SS7.3. Cumulated educational spending versus 2006 PISA mathematics scores

Source: OECD (2008), *Education at a Glance*, OECD, Paris (*www.oecd.org/edu/EAG2008*).

StatLink http://dx.doi.org/10.1787/550244873353

6. EQUITY INDICATORS

1. Income inequality

2. Poverty

3. Poverty among children

4. Adequacy of benefits of last resort

5. Public social spending

6. Total social spending

Definition and measurement

Measures of income inequality are based on data on people's household disposable income. Disposable income is gross household income following deduction of direct taxes and payment of social security contributions. It excludes in-kind services provided to households by governments and private entities, consumption taxes, and imputed income flows due to home ownership and other real assets. People are attributed the income of the household to which they belong. Household income is adjusted to take account of household size by assuming a common equivalence scale of 0.5. The main indicator of income distribution used is the Gini coefficient. Values of the Gini coefficient range between 0 in the case of "perfect equality" (each person gets the same income) and 1 in the case of "perfect inequality" (all income goes to the share of the population with the highest income). An inter-decile income ratio, the ratio between the upper limit of the 9th decile and that of the 1st decile, is also used.

The data used here are provided to the OECD by national consultants. They are based on common methodologies and definitions applied to national micro data sets. While this approach improves cross-country comparability, national data sets do differ from one another in ways that are not readily standardised.

Income inequality varies considerably across the OECD countries. In the mid-2000s, the Gini coefficient of income inequality was lowest in Denmark and Sweden and highest in Mexico and Turkey (EQ1.1). The Gini coefficient for the most unequal country is double the value of the most equal country. The P90/P10 inter-decile ratio also shows large disparities, with the income top decile less than three times higher than that of the bottom decile in Denmark, Sweden and Norway but around six times higher in the United States, Portugal and Turkey, and more than eight times higher in Mexico. The correlation between the two summary measures of income inequality used in EQ1.1 is high (above 0.95).

Income inequality has generally been rising. From a policy perspective changes in income distribution across countries, rather than level comparisons, are more relevant. Figure EQ1.2 shows point changes in the Gini coefficient over three different time periods. Over the entire period from the mid-1980s to the mid-2000s (right panel of EQ1.2), inequality rises in 19 out of 24 countries where data were available. Rising inequality is strongest in Finland, New Zealand and Portugal. Declines occur in France, Greece, and Turkey, as well as Ireland and Spain (where data are limited to 2000) . The OECD average increase in the Gini coefficient is equivalent to a hypothetical 4% transfer of average income from people in the lower half of the distribution to people in the upper half. Overall, this growth in inequality is moderate but significant.

Income inequality rose during the period from the late 1980s to the mid-1990s across many countries, and thereafter the pattern was more diverse. The centre and left panels of EQ1.2 show significant differences in inequality trends across both countries and periods. In the decade from the mid-1980s to the mid-1990s (left panel), the dominant pattern of rising inequality is especially evident in Mexico, New Zealand and Turkey, as well as in several other countries. There is more diversity in inequality change in the following decade (central panel). Higher inequality is found in many countries – especially in Canada, Finland, Germany, Norway, Portugal, Sweden and the United States. Over that period there have been large inequality declines in Mexico and Turkey and smaller ones in Australia, Greece, Ireland, the Netherlands and the United Kingdom.

Further reading

OECD (2008), *Growing Unequal – Income Distribution and Poverty in OECD Countries*, OECD, Paris (*www.oecd.org/ els/social/inequality*).

Figure notes

Figure EQ1.1: Countries are ranked, from left to right, in increasing order in the Gini coefficient. The income concept used is that of disposable household income in cash, adjusted for household size with an elasticity of 0.5.

Figure EQ1.2: In the first panel, data refer to changes from around 1990 to the mid-1990s for the Czech Republic, Hungary and Portugal and to the western Länder of Germany (no data are available for Australia, Poland and Switzerland). In the second panel, data refer to changes from the mid-1990s to around 2000 for Austria, the Czech Republic, Belgium, Ireland, Portugal and Spain (where 2005 data, based on EU-SILC, are not deemed to be comparable with those for earlier years). OECD-24 refers to the simple average of OECD countries with data spanning the entire period (all countries shown above except Australia); OECD-22 excludes Mexico and Turkey.

EQ1.1. Income inequality varies considerably across OECD countries

Gini coefficient and inter-decile ratio (P90/P10), mid-2000s

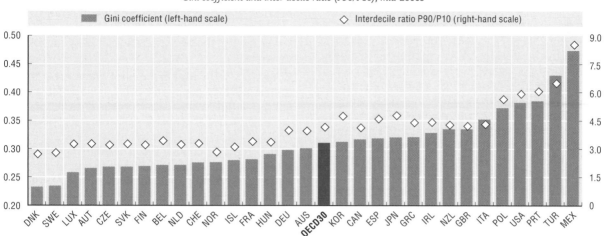

EQ1.2. Income inequality has generally been rising

Percentage point changes in the Gini coefficient

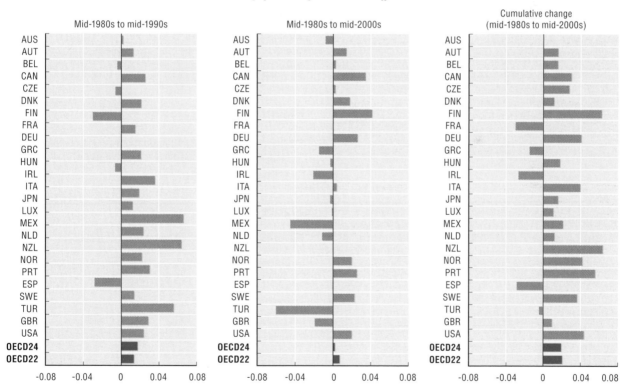

Source: OECD (2008), *Growing Unequal: Income Distribution and Poverty
in OECD Countries*, OECD, Paris (*www.oecd.org/els/social/inequality*).

StatLink ᗧᔙᣤ http://dx.doi.org/10.1787/550365522422

Definition and measurement

Avoiding material hardship is a primary objective of social policy, sometimes made explicit though a constitutional right to a decent standard of living. However, perceptions of "a decent standard of living" vary across countries and over time. Hence no commonly agreed measure of poverty across OECD countries exists. As with income inequality, the starting point for poverty measurement is equivalised household disposable income provided by national consultants (see "Definition and measurement" under EQ1. Income inequality). People are classified as poor when their equivalised household income is less than half of the median prevailing in each country. The use of a relative income-threshold means that richer countries have the higher poverty thresholds. Higher poverty thresholds in richer countries capture the notion that avoiding poverty means an ability to access to the goods and services that are regarded as "customary" in any given county.

Poverty is considered in terms of the poverty rate and poverty gap. The poverty rate is a headcount of how many people fall below the poverty line. The poverty gap measures the extent to which the income of the poor falls below the poverty line. The poverty gap is the mean aggregate income shortfall relative to the poverty line.

The average OECD country poverty rate was 11% in the mid-2000s (EQ2.1). There is considerable diversity in country experiences. Poverty rates are around 15% in Poland, Korea, Ireland and Japan, and 17-18% in Mexico, Turkey, and the United States, while they are below 6% in Denmark, Sweden and the Czech Republic. Different thresholds change poverty rates considerably. Based on a threshold set at 40% of median income, the average OECD poverty rate falls to around 6%. The average poverty rate rises to around 17% for a threshold of 60% of median income.

The OECD average poverty gap was 29% in the mid-2000s (EQ2.1). The poverty gap is largest in Mexico, the United States and Switzerland, with a shortfall around 38%. At the lower end, in Finland, Luxembourg, the Netherlands and Belgium, it hovers around 20%.

Countries with higher poverty rates tend to have higher poverty gaps. The two measurements have a solid positive correlation of 0.60. Within this broad tendency, there are some notable outliers. Poverty gaps are well above OECD average, at 30% or more, in some of the countries characterised by relatively low poverty rates, such as Iceland and Switzerland in particular. Equally, poverty gaps are below average for some countries like Australia, Canada, Greece and Ireland which have higher than OECD average poverty rates.

Poverty rates generally increased over the period from mid-1980 to mid-2000s (EQ2.2). Rates fell for eight countries and rose for 16 countries. The biggest falls were registered in Belgium and Mexico, whereas the other countries had small poverty declines of around one percentage point or less. The largest rises, between 4 and 5 percentage points, were experienced by Germany, Ireland, the Netherlands and New Zealand. There is no clear pattern of difference of poverty rises between the mid-1980s and mid-1990s and the mid-1990s to the mid-2000s. The increase was about 0.6 points in each sub-period.

Further reading

OECD (2008), *Growing Unequal – Income Distribution and Poverty in OECD Countries*, OECD, Paris (*www.oecd.org/els/social/inequality*).

Figure note

Figure EQ2.2: Data in the left figure refer to changes in the poverty headcount from around 1990 to mid-1990s for Czech Republic, Hungary and Portugal; no data are available for Australia and Switzerland. Data in the middle figure refer to changes from the mid-1990s to around 2000 for Austria, Belgium, Czech Republic, Ireland, Portugal and Spain (where 2005 data, based on EU-SILC, are not comparable with those for earlier years); and to changes from 2000 to 2005 for Switzerland. OECD24 refers to the simple average of OECD countries with data spanning the entire period (all countries shown above except Australia and Switzerland).

EQ2.1. OECD countries with high poverty rates tend to have high poverty gaps

Poverty rate and poverty gap, mid-2000s, 50% poverty threshold

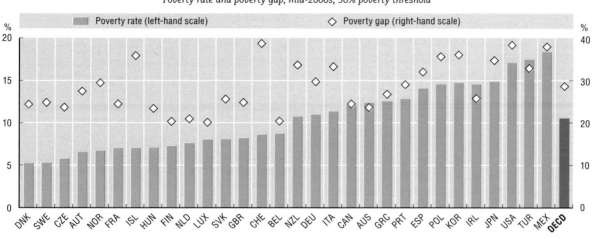

EQ2.2. Poverty rates generally increased over the period from mid-1980s to mid-2000s

Percentage point changes in income poverty rate at 50% median level over different time periods

Source: OECD (2008), *Growing Unequal: Income Distribution and Poverty in OECD Countries*, OECD, Paris (www.oecd.org/els/social/inequality).

StatLink ᴍᴌᴴ http://dx.doi.org/10.1787/550406285615

3. Poverty among children

Definition and measurement

Children are defined as poor when they live in households whose equivalised disposable income is less than 50% of the median of a given country (see "Definition and measurement" for EQ1. Income inequality). Children, defined as all those aged under 18, are considered as sharing the income earned by other household members. The basic indicator of child poverty used here in the poverty rate, measured as the share of children with an equivalised income of less than 50% of the median. Also shown are the poverty rates for all people living in households with children (i.e. including adult members).

More than for other age groups, estimates of child poverty are sensitive to the value of the equivalence scale elasticity. Estimates shown here may also count some students (aged 18 or less) living away of the parental home as poor children. Further, as the data used here retain the household as the basic unit where income is polled and shared, they do not capture biological and social relationships between household members. As a result, people classified as "single adult with children" will include, beyond sole parents, other household arrangements (such as a grandparent living with his or her nephew). Similarly, "couples with children" may include some single parent families sharing their housing with other adults.

Poverty among children is of special concern across the OECD. Children have little control over the material situation of their families. In addition the experience of poverty during childhood may adversely affect a child's cognitive and social development into adulthood.

The average OECD child poverty rate was 12% in the mid 2000s (EQ3.1, left-hand panel). Child poverty rates are below 5% in Denmark, Finland, Sweden and Norway, and below 8% in France and Austria. Child poverty exceeds 20% in the United States, Poland, Mexico and Turkey.

Poverty rates for children generally exceed population poverty rates. Countries where children are less likely to be poor than the general population include Australia, Austria, Denmark, Finland, Japan, Korea, Norway, and Sweden. On the other hand, child poverty is higher by 3 points or more in Canada, the Czech Republic, Germany, Italy, Luxembourg, Mexico, New Zealand, Poland, Portugal, Spain, Turkey and the United States.

Child poverty rates have risen in the last decade across the OECD. The small rise is despite announcements of child poverty targets in several OECD countries and introduction of other policies focused on reducing numbers of poor children. Large rises in child poverty have taken place in Turkey, Germany, Luxembourg and Austria. Significant declines are found in Mexico, Italy and the United Kingdom (EQ3.1, right-hand panel).

Children in sole parent families and in families without work are more likely to be poor (EQ3.2). A considerable amount of the association of sole parenthood with child poverty is because sole parents lack work. If work is lacking, average OECD rates of poverty in sole parent families with children are similar to rates of poverty in two parent families with children. Poverty rates are also slightly elevated when there are more children in the family.

Further reading

OECD (2008), *Growing Unequal – Income Distribution and Poverty in OECD Countries*, OECD, Paris (*www.oecd.org/els/social/inequality*).

Figure and table notes

Figure EQ3.1: Countries are ranked, from top to bottom, in decreasing order of the poverty rate in mid-2000s.

Table EQ3.2: Changes refer to 1995-2000 for Austria, Belgium, Czech Republic, Ireland, Portugal and Spain, and to 2000-05 for Switzerland. For France, levels refer to EU-SILC, changes to Enquête revenus fiscaux (ERF).

EQ3.1. Child poverty rates across the OECD rose slightly in the last decade

Poverty rates based on a 50% of median income threshold in percent, and percentage point changes in poverty rates

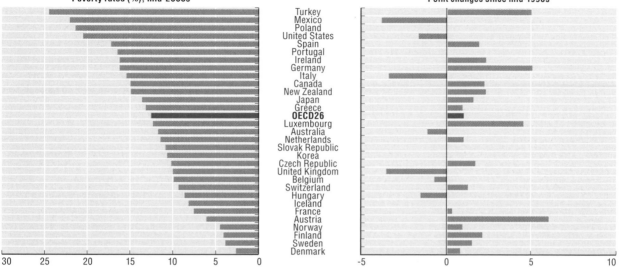

Poverty rates (%), mid-2000s

Point changes since mid-1990s

EQ3.2. Children in sole parent families and in families without work are more likely to be poor

Poverty rates based on a 50% of median income threshold in percent, and percentage point changes in poverty rates

	Poverty among children		Poverty in households with children and a head of working age									
			All		Single		Couple			By number of children		
	Mid-2000s	Point changes since mid-1990s	Level, mid-2000s	change from 1995	Not working	Working	No workers	One worker	Two and more workers	One	Two	Three and more
							Level, mid-2000s					
Australia	12	−1.2	10	−1.0	68	6	51	8	1	9	10	11
Austria	6	6.0	6	6.1	51	11	36	4	3	6	5	6
Belgium	10	−0.8	9	0.1	43	10	36	11	3	7	9	11
Canada	15	2.2	13	1.6	89	32	81	22	4	11	13	18
Czech Republic	10	1.7	8	1.4	71	10	43	9	1	8	6	[. .]
Denmark	3	0.8	2	0.7	20	4	21	5	0	2	2	4
Finland	4	2.1	4	1.9	46	6	23	9	1	5	3	3
France	8	0.3	7	−0.2	46	12	48	12	2	6	7	10
Germany	16	5.1	13	4.2	56	26	47	6	1	13	13	14
Greece	13	0.9	12	0.9	84	18	39	22	4	8	13	19
Hungary	9	−1.6	8	−1.1	44	16	22	6	3	5	6	14
Iceland	8	. .	7	. .	23	17	51	29	4	7	6	10
Ireland	16	2.3	14	. .	75	24	55	16	2	12	12	19
Italy	16	−3.4	14	−3.1	[. .]	16	78	24	1	. .	. .	. .
Japan	14	1.6	12	1.2	60	58	50	11	10	. .	. .	. .
Korea	11	. .	10	. .	32	25	59	11	4	. .	. .	. .
Luxembourg	12	4.5	11	3.8	69	38	27	16	5	7	13	14
Mexico	22	−3.8	19	−2.4	30	34	53	27	11	11	16	26
Netherlands	12	1.0	9	1.2	62	27	65	12	2	. .	. .	. .
New Zealand	15	2.3	13	1.5	48	30	47	21	3	. .	. .	. .
Norway	5	0.9	4	0.6	31	5	29	4	0	4	2	6
Poland	22	. .	19	. .	75	26	51	28	6	15	18	31
Portugal	17	0.0	14	0.4	[. .]	26	53	34	5	10	17	[. .]
Slovak Republic	11	. .	10	. .	66	24	66	18	2	. .	. .	. .
Spain	17	1.9	15	1.1	78	32	71	23	5	10	16	29
Sweden	4	1.5	4	1.5	18	6	36	14	1	4	3	3
Switzerland	9	1.2	6	1.3	22			8	. .	. .	. .	
Turkey	25	5.0	20	3.6	44	32	28	19	20	. .	. .	. .
United Kingdom	10	−3.6	9	−3.7	39	7	36	9	1	4	6	20
United States	21	−1.7	18	−1.1	92	36	82	27	6	14	15	26
OECD	**12**	**1.0**	**11**	**0.8**	**54**	**21**	**48**	**16**	**4**	**8**	**10**	**15**

Source: OECD (2008), *Growing Unequal: Income Distribution and Poverty in OECD Countries*, OECD, Paris (*www.oecd.org/els/social/inequality*).

StatLink ⇩ http://dx.doi.org/10.1787/550407525853

Definition and measurement

Compared to after-tax incomes from employment, net incomes of benefit recipients measure the financial incentives to take up work for those without a job. When compared to the income cut-off points that are used to identify poor families, they inform about the capacity of benefit systems to ensure an adequate standard of living.

The indicators shown below for two different periods (2001 and 2005, the latter period chosen to draw on data from *Growing Unequal*) use the OECD tax-benefit models to compare net incomes of two different sole-parent family types against cut-off levels used to measure income poverty (40, 50 and 60% of median household income). Both sole parent families have two children aged 6 and 4. In the first case no unemployment benefit is received and no labour market income is earned. The only sources of family income are therefore family-related cash benefits as well as "last resort" social assistance payments. The family relies on benefits for the entire tax year. The second set of results shows incomes for the same family but with the parent in a full-time minimum-wage job. All income measures are net of taxes but do not account for work-related costs such as for childcare. Median household incomes for both years are taken from *Growing Unequal*. The OECD publication *Benefits and Wages* (2007) provides further details on methodology.

Benefits of last resort are often set below the thresholds conventionally used in making poverty comparisons across the OECD (EQ4.1). Benefit recipients unable to earn income face considerable poverty risks in all OECD countries. In all but 11 of the 26 OECD countries considered the 2005 incomes of jobless sole parents were below a 50% poverty threshold. Nine countries were at or above a 50% threshold in 2001.

Amounts of social assistance and associated benefits have generally slightly increased in effectiveness in reducing sole parent poverty over the period 2001-05. The fall in effectiveness with respect to sole parent poverty reduction is normally not on account of nominal benefits being reduced, but because median household incomes rise faster than benefits. If benefits are adjusted with low temporal frequency with different cycles across countries, this could account for some of the country differences in changes in effectiveness.

For those sole parents taking up employment from benefits of last resort, full-time low-wage work can bring solid income gains. Figure EQ4.2 shows that a full-time minimum wage job takes sole parent families out of poverty defined as 50% of median income in Australia, Belgium, Ireland, Japan, the Netherlands, New Zealand, Poland, and the United Kingdom. Effectiveness of the minimum wage in sole parent poverty alleviation conditional on full-time work is rising most in Poland, Ireland, and Hungary and falling most in Australia, the United Kingdom and New Zealand. As with benefit patterns through time, the variability could reflect timing of minimum wage adjustments.

Combining adequate safety-nets with strong work incentives requires a carefully balanced system. Figure EQ4.3 indicates that Australia, Ireland and the United Kingdom pay relatively high benefits to sole parents while at the same time maintaining relatively strong work incentives for moving from benefits of last resort into full-time minimum wage work.

Further reading

OECD (2007), *Benefits and Wages: OECD Indicators*, OECD, Paris.

OECD (2008), *Growing Unequal – Income Distribution and Poverty in OECD Countries*, OECD, Paris.

Figure notes

Figure EQ4.1: Italy and Turkey have no generally applicable benefits of last resort for sole parents. The shaded area represents the area between the different poverty thresholds defined as 40, 50 and 60% of median household income. Net incomes include housing-related benefits. Figures at the bottom of each bar refer to the 2005 rate.

Figure EQ4.2: The countries which are in EQ4.1 but are missing from missing from EQ4.2 have no statutory minimum wage. Net incomes include housing-related benefits. Figures at the bottom of each bar refer to the 2005 rate.

EQ4.1. Sole parent families with no market income face high poverty risks in some countries

Net income solely on social assistance for sole parents with two children/median equivalent household income

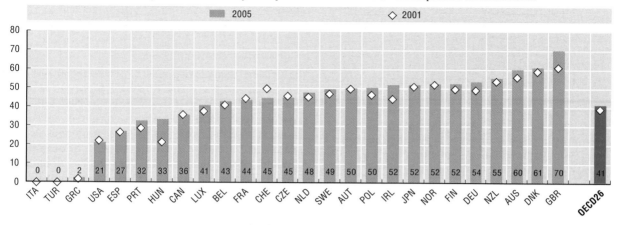

EQ4.2. Supporting full-time work can reduce poverty, even when the job is only paid the minimum wage

Net income for sole parents with two children working full-time on the minimum wage/median equivalent household income

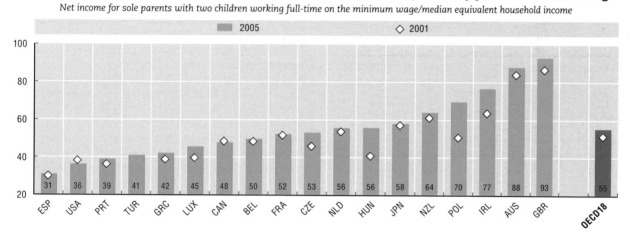

EQ4.3. Some countries succeed in combining stronger work incentives with adequate safety nets for sole parents

Percentage point difference between income in full-time minimum wage work and benefits of last resort relative to median income, compared to benefits of last resort relative to median income, sole parents with two children

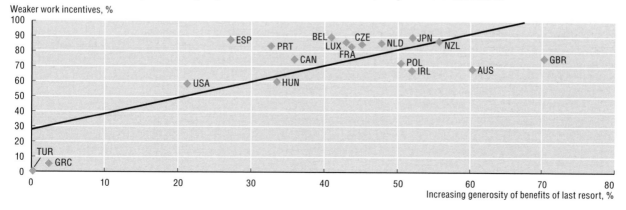

Source: OECD tax-benefit model (*www.oecd.org/els/social/workincentives*).   *StatLink* ᴍ᎒ᔕᴿ http://dx.doi.org/10.1787/550413205665

Definition and measurement

Social support to those in need is provided by a wide range of people and social institutions through a variety of means. Much of this support takes the form of social expenditures, which comprises both financial support (through cash benefits and tax advantages) and "in-kind" provision of goods and services. To be included in social spending, benefits have to address one or more contingencies, such as low-income, old-age, unemployment and disability.

Social expenditure is classified as public when general government (i.e. central administration, local governments and social security institutions) controls the financial flows. For example, sickness benefits financed by compulsory contributions from employers and employees to social insurance funds are considered "public", whereas sickness benefits paid directly by employers to their employees are classified as "private". For cross-country comparisons, the indicator of social spending used here refers to public spending as a share of Net National Income. The spending flows shown here are recorded on before deduction of direct and indirect tax payments levied on these benefits and before addition of tax expenditures provided for social purposes ("gross spending"). Spending by lower tiers of government may be underestimated in some countries, especially more decentralised or federal polities.

In 2005, gross public social expenditure was on average 24% of NNI across 30 OECD countries (EQ5.1). Cross country differences in spending levels are wide. Mexico and Korea spend 8% of NNI while Sweden spends 26 percentage points of NNI more. Sweden is closely followed by France, Luxembourg and Austria in terms of spending shares. In terms of cash transfers, these latter three countries spend considerably more than Sweden (as do others). A considerable number of countries cluster relatively tightly, just above and – particularly – just below the OECD average.

Cash benefits were larger than in-kind services in 25 countries. In Poland, Italy and Austria cash benefits exceeded in-kind benefits by at least 10 percentage points of NNI, while in Iceland, Canada and Mexico, services dominate, being at least 3 percentage points of NNI higher than cash benefits.

The three largest categories of public social spending are pensions (9% of NNI on average), health (7%) and income transfers to the working-aged (5%). Pension spending accounts for more than 12% of NNI in Austria, France, Germany, Greece, Italy, and Poland, and less than 5% in Australia, Canada, Iceland, Ireland, Korea, and Mexico. Gross public spending on social services exceeds 5% of NNI only in Denmark, Norway and Iceland.

Public social spending has been increasing as a share of NNI in the last generation and converging across OECD countries (EQ5.2). The overall rise has been on average 5 percentage points. Most of this average gain occurred during the period 1980-92. Thereafter there is less evidence of a time trend. The left panel of Figure EQ5.2 shows developments for selected high spenders, and the right panel shows developments for selected low spenders. Post-1992 stabilisation in spending shares seems to have come more strongly from the high spenders, with considerable falls in spending after 1992, in particular for Sweden. On the other hand the lower spending countries show a more steadily rising trend throughout the period. The upshot of such a pattern is a growing convergence in social spending patterns across the OECD, at least in terms of NNI shares.

Figure notes

Figure EQ5.1: Countries are ranked by decreasing order of public social expenditure as a percentage of NNI. Spending on Active Labour Market Programmes (ALMPs) cannot be split by cash/services breakdown; they are however included in the total public spending (shown in brackets). 2004 data for Portugal.

Figure EQ5.2: Information for 1980 to 2005 is available for 23 countries, while information for the Czech Republic, Iceland, Korea, Mexico, and Poland is available for 1990 onwards. OECD-30 refers to an unweighted average of OECD countries, not including Hungary (data from 1999 onwards) and Slovak Republic (data from 1995 onwards). 2005 data for Portugal refers to 2004.

SOCIETY AT A GLANCE 2009: OECD SOCIAL INDICATORS – ISBN 978-92-64-04938-3 – © OECD 2009

EQ5.1. On average public social spending accounts for one fourth of NNI across OECD countries

Public social expenditure by broad social policy area, in percentage of NNI, 2005

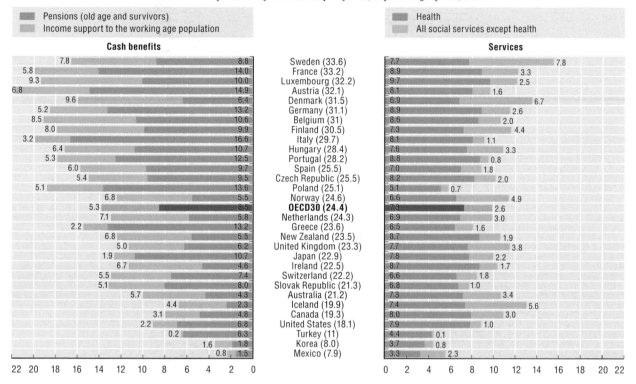

Cash benefits		Services
▓ Pensions (old age and survivors)		▓ Health
░ Income support to the working age population		░ All social services except health

EQ5.2. Upward trends in public social spending-to-NNI ratio

Public social spending for selected countries, 1980-2005, in percentage of NNI

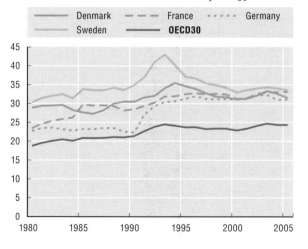

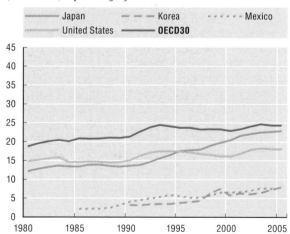

Source: OECD (2008), *Social Expenditure Database, 1980-2005*
(www.oecd.org/els/social/expenditure).

StatLink http://dx.doi.org/10.1787/550420773523

Definition and measurement

A comprehensive account of the total amount of resources that each OECD country devotes to social support has to account both public and private social expenditures, and the extent to which the tax system affects the effective amount of support provided. To capture the effect of the tax system on gross, before tax social expenditures, account should be taken of the government claw back through the direct taxation of benefit-income and the indirect taxation of the goods and services consumed by benefit recipients. Moreover, governments can pursue social goals via tax breaks for social purposes (e.g. child tax allowances), which tends to make total social spending in excess of gross spending. From a social perspective of society, net after tax social expenditure, from both public and private sources, gives a better indication of the resources committed to social goals.

As administrative data are frequently not available, measuring the impact of the tax system on social expenditure often requires estimates derived from micro-data sets and micro simulation models. Also central recording of private social spending is not always available. Hence there is likely to be more error in this data than for data on public social expenditure (see EQ5).

On average 13% of gross social spending was clawed back in net taxes across the OECD in 2005 (EQ6.1). However, the amount clawed back in net taxation is variable, meaning that a ranking of countries by gross spending may be quite different from a net spending ranking. There are several features which stand out in considering patterns of impacts of tax payments and tax credits on gross social spending by governments in selected OECD countries. First, the claw back of gross social spending through direct taxation of bene-fit income is highest in the Nordic welfare states of Denmark, Finland and Sweden, where between one fifth and one quarter of gross spending returns to the government coffers. Second, net public social spending in Mexico, the United States and Korea is greater than gross spending (in Canada they are equal in value). In fact the excess of net over gross public social spending in Mexico rivals the shortfall of net over gross spending in the three Nordic countries by a similar proportional absolute amount.

Across 26 OECD countries, average net public social expenditure accounted for 25% of NNI. The range was from 9% in Korea up to 33% in Germany and 35% in France. Low gross spending countries have more tax breaks at the bottom end and the high gross spending Nordics claw back considerable amounts in taxation. Thus accounting for both private social benefits and the impact of the tax system considerably reduces country differences in social spending ratios across countries. However, a more similar net social spend across countries does not imply that the degree of redistribution achieved through the tax and benefit systems is also similar, since these are simple country-wide averages which provide no indication of who gets what.

Total net social spending across the OECD, including private spending, is 28% of NNI (EQ6.2). Consideration of private spending adds another 3 percentage points of NNI on average. The big mover up the country rankings from inclusion of private social spending is the United States, which is the third lowest spender in terms of public social spending but which rises above the OECD average to spend 31% of NNI. The cause is the addition of 10 percentage points of private spending.

Figure and table notes

Table EQ6.1: – Zero; . . Data not available.

Figure EQ6.2: Countries are ranked in decreasing order of total net social spending; since adjustments are required for indirect taxation, net social spending is related to NNI at factor costs rather than to NNI at market prices.

EQ6.1. From gross to net public social spending
Percentage of NNI at factor costs, 2005

	Australia	Austria	Belgium	Canada	Czech Republic	Denmark	Finland	France	Germany	Iceland	Ireland	Italy	Japan	Korea	Luxembourg	Mexico	Netherlands	New Zealand	Norway	Poland	Portugal	Slovak Republic	Spain	Sweden	United Kingdom	United States	OECD26
Gross public social expenditure	24.5	36.9	35.9	22.2	29.0	38.3	32.7	39.3	35.5	24.6	26.7	35.2	24.1	9.2	38.4	9.0	28.1	28.0	27.8	29.6	33.5	24.7	29.3	40.5	26.9	19.6	**28.8**
− Direct taxes and social contributions on benefit income	0.3	3.3	1.9	0.5	0.0	5.7	3.5	1.9	1.8	1.0	0.3	2.7	0.3	0.0	1.3	–	3.1	1.9	2.3	2.2	1.1	–	1.6	5.5	0.3	0.6	**1.8**
− Indirect taxes on goods and services consumed by benefit recipients	1.1	3.6	3.2	1.0	3.0	3.9	3.6	3.3	2.6	1.6	2.9	2.6	0.8	0.5	4.9	0.2	2.2	2.0	2.7	3.4	3.3	2.6	2.2	3.2	1.7	0.4	**2.4**
+ Tax breaks towards non-pension social policy spending	0.5	0.1	0.6	1.5	0.7	0.0	–	1.3	2.3	–	0.6	0.3	1.0	0.7	0.0	1.8	1.0	0.1	0.1	0.1	1.2	0.1	0.6	–	0.5	2.5	**0.8**
= Net public social expenditure	23.6	30.1	31.5	22.3	26.7	28.8	25.6	35.3	33.4	22.1	24.2	30.3	24.0	9.5	32.1	10.6	23.8	24.2	23.0	24.2	30.4	22.2	26.1	31.9	25.5	21.1	**25.5**
Memorandum item																											
Tax breaks towards pensions	2.8	0.1	0.2	2.3	0.2	..	0.2	0.0	1.2	1.5	2.2	0.0	0.1	..	..	0.1	..	..	0.8	0.3	0.1	0.2	0.4	0.0	1.6	1.0	..

EQ6.2. From public to total net social spending
Percentage of NNI at factor costs, 2005

Legend: Gross expenditure ▮ / Net expenditure ▮

	A. Public social expenditure		B. Total (public + private) social expenditure	
	Gross	Net	Gross	Net
France	39.3	35.3	39.0	43.3
Belgium	35.9	31.5	36.4	42.1
Germany	35.5	33.4	35.8	39.5
Sweden	40.5	31.9	34.2	44.3
Luxembourg	38.4	32.1	33.6	40.2
United Kingdom	26.9	25.5	32.8	36.0
Italy	35.2	30.3	32.5	38.1
Netherlands	28.1	24.7	32.0	39.5
Austria	36.9	30.1	31.4	34.8
Denmark	38.3	28.8	31.3	39.3
United States	19.6	21.1	31.1	32.1
Portugal	33.5	30.4	30.7	42.0
OECD26	28.8	25.5	28.4	32.8
Japan	24.1	24.0	28.3	28.9
Canada	22.2	22.3	27.8	29.6
Australia	24.5	23.6	27.6	29.8
Czech Republic	29.0	26.7	27.1	29.6
Iceland	24.6	22.1	26.9	31.8
Finland	32.7	25.6	26.6	34.2
Spain	29.3	26.1	26.3	30.0
Ireland	26.7	24.2	25.7	28.9
New Zealand	28.0	24.2	24.7	28.6
Norway	27.8	23.0	24.5	30.5
Poland	29.6	24.2	24.2	29.7
Slovak Republic	24.7	22.2	23.4	26.2
Korea	9.2	9.5	12.7	12.6
Mexico	9.0	10.6	10.8	9.2

Source: OECD (2008), *Social Expenditure Database, 1980-2005*
(*www.oecd.org/els/social/expenditure*).

StatLink ⟶ http://dx.doi.org/10.1787/550438273480

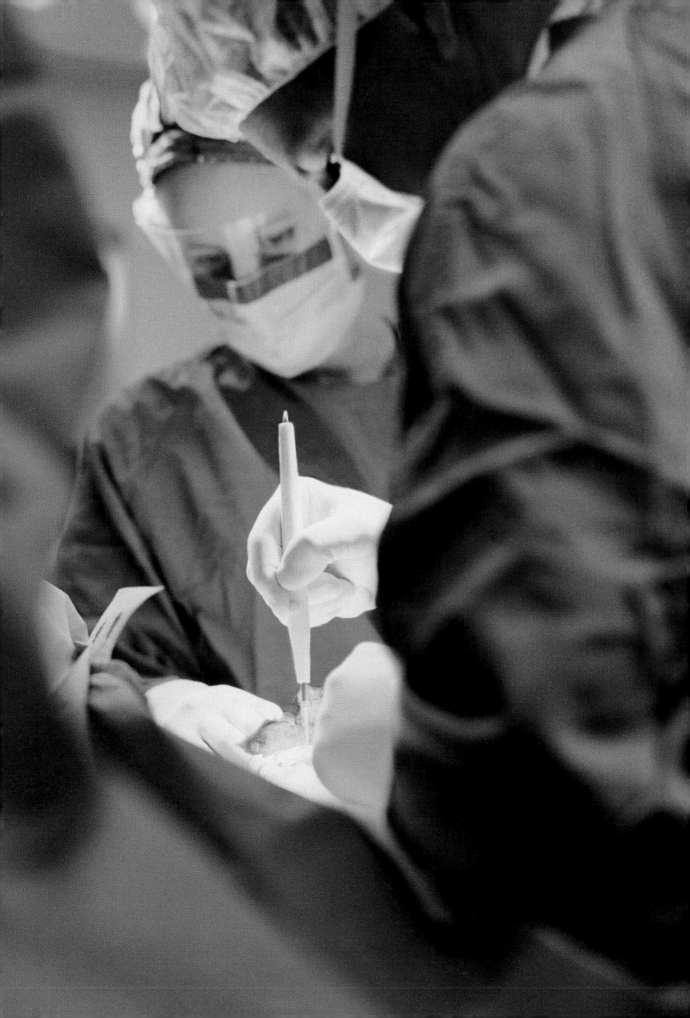

7. HEALTH INDICATORS

1. Life expectancy

2. Perceived health status

3. Infant health

4. Obesity

5. Height

6. Mental health

7. Long-term care recipients

8. Health care expenditure

Life expectancy at birth has increased remarkably in OECD countries. From 1960 average OECD female life expectancy at birth increased by 10.9 years to a level of 81.7 years in 2006. For men the increase was of 10.2 years to 76.0 years (HE1.1). In 2006, life expectancy at birth among women was highest in Japan (85.8 years), followed by France, Spain, Switzerland and Italy. For men, life expectancy was highest in Iceland (79.4 years) followed by Switzerland, Japan, Australia and Sweden.

The increase in life expectancy was accompanied by a large reduction in cross-country differences. In Korea and Turkey, life expectancy at birth for women and men combined increased by 26.7 and 23.3 years respectively between 1960 and 2006, while in Mexico the gain exceeded 18 years. Catch-up gains in life expectancy by these countries mainly reflect a significant convergence in infant mortality rates.

There is little evidence that increases in life expectancy are approaching a ceiling. Gains in life expectancy at birth for Japanese women halved after the period of catching-up, but have since continued at a rate of around 3% per year.

The gender gap in life expectancy has widened slightly. Since gains in life expectancy at birth since 1960 have been greater for women than for men, the average OECD gender gap in life expectancy widened from 5.0 years in 1960 to 5.7 years in 2006. However, there have been different trends between earlier and later decades. While the gender gap in life expectancy increased substantially during the 1960s and 1970s (to a peak of 6.7 years, on average, in 1980), it has narrowed during the past 25 years. This narrowing reflects, in part, the lower differences in the prevalence of risk-factor behaviours (e.g. smoking) between men and women and lower mortality rates from cardiovascular disease among men.

Old people are living longer. Life expectancy at older ages has also increased substantially thanks to improved access to health services and medical progress, especially in the treatment of cardiovascular diseases. In 2006, on average, women aged 65 could expect to live an additional 20.1 years, up by 5.3 years since 1960. Men of the same age could expect to live 16.7 more years, with a gain of 4.0 years since 1960 (HE1.2). Gender gaps in longevity in old age have narrowed in several OECD countries since the mid-1980s, and this trend is projected to continue in the future.

Overall longevity gains are due to rising living standards, better nutrition, less smoking and drinking, and better education, as well as greater access to quality health services. However, gains in life expectancy have been smaller among people from lower socioeconomic groups (OECD, 2004).

Further reading

OECD (2004), *Towards High-performing Health Systems*, OECD, Paris.

Figure note

Figure HE1.2: 2005 for Canada, United Kingdom and United States. 2004 for Italy.

HE1.1. Life expectancy at birth has increased remarkably in OECD countries

Life expectancy at birth, in years, men and women, in 1960 and 2006

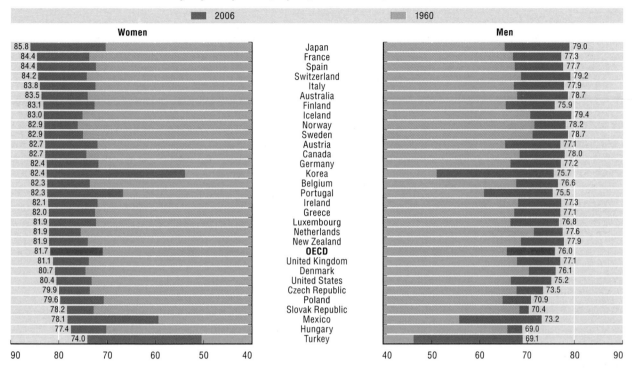

HE1.2. Older people have a considerable life expectancy

Life expectancy at 65, in years, men and women, in 2006

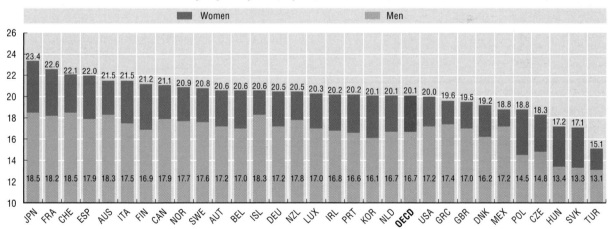

Source: OECD (2008), *OECD Health Data 2008*, CD-Rom, OECD, Paris (*www.oecd.org/health/healthdata*).

StatLink ⫍⫥⫤⫢ http://dx.doi.org/10.1787/550470572014

Definition and measurement

Most OECD countries conduct regular health interview surveys asking variants of the question "How is your health in general? Very good, good, fair, poor, very poor". Despite the general and subjective nature of this question, indicators of perceived health status have been found to be a good predictor of people's future health care use and mortality (Miilunpalo *et al.*, 1997).

Caution is required in making cross-country comparisons of perceived health status, for two reasons. First, people's assessment of their health can be affected by a number of factors beyond their "real" health status, such as cultural background. Second, there are variations in the question and answer categories used to measure perceived health across surveys/countries. In particular, the response scale used in the United States, Canada, New Zealand and Australia is skewed on the positive side via including the five response categories: "excellent, very good, good, fair, poor". The data reported refer to respondents answering one of the three positive responses ("excellent", "very good" or "good"). By contrast, in most other OECD countries, the response scale is symmetric, with response categories being: "very good", "good", "fair", "poor", "very poor". The data reported from these countries refer only to the first two categories ("very good" and "good").

Most people think their health is good. In half of OECD countries, 75% or more of the adult population rate their health to be good or very good or excellent (HE2.1). New Zealand, the United States and Canada are the three countries that have the highest proportion of people assessing their health to be good or very good, with about nine out of ten people reporting to be in good health. This good performance could be a data artefact (see "Definition and measurement" above). In Mexico, Spain and Finland, about two-thirds of the adult population rate their health to be good or very good. At the lower end of the scale, less than half of the adult population in the Slovak Republic, Japan, Portugal, Hungary and Korea rate their health to be good or very good.

Men think they are healthier than women. In the majority of countries, men are more likely than women to rate their health as good or better (HE2.2). Unsurprisingly, people's positive rating of their own health declines with age. In many countries, there is a particularly marked decline in a positive rating of one's own health after age 45 and a further decline after age 65. In all OECD countries, people with a lower level of education and people with a lower level of income do not rate their health as positively as people with better education or higher income.

Proportions of people reporting good health are stable over time. In countries with a long time series, the proportion of the adult population rating their health as being good or very good has not changed over the past 25 years (HE2.3). The same is true for the population aged 65 and over. One interpretation of the coexistence of relatively stable rates of perceived health status among the population with the steady rise in life expectancy over the past 25 years is that people are living longer, but not necessarily healthier. Another explanation may be that people adapt, so as health increases, so does people's perception of what being healthy means.

Further reading

Miilunpalo, S. *et al.* (1997), "Self-rated Health Status as a Health Measure: The Predictive Value of Self-reported Health Status on the Use of Physician Services and on Mortality in the Working-age Population", *Journal of Clinical Epidemiology*, Vol. 50, No. 5, pp. 517-528.

Figure notes

Figures HE2.1 and HE2.2: Note 1: Results for these countries are not directly comparable with those for other countries, due to methodological differences in the survey questionnaire resulting in an upward bias.

HE2.1. Most people think their health is good

Percentage of population aged 15 and over reporting good health

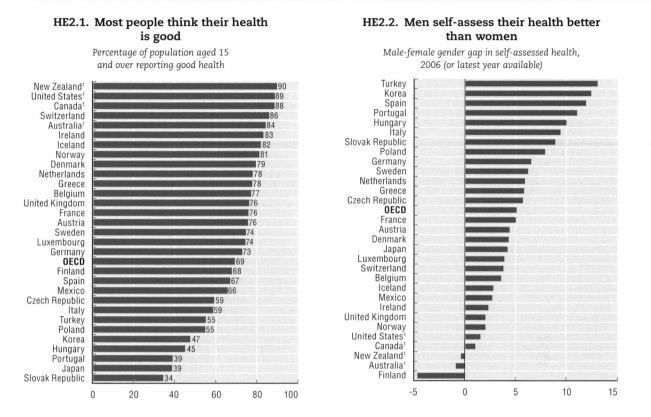

HE2.2. Men self-assess their health better than women

Male-female gender gap in self-assessed health, 2006 (or latest year available)

HE2.3. Proportions of people reporting good health are stable over long time periods

Percentage of population aged 15 and over reporting good health

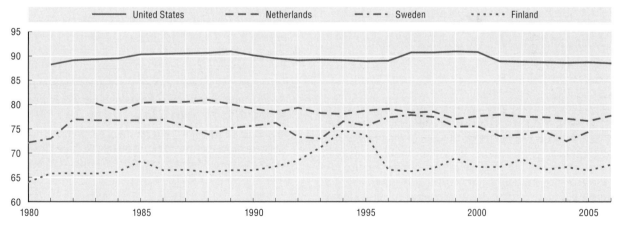

Source: OECD (2008), OECD Health Data 2008, CD-Rom, OECD, Paris (www.oecd.org/health/healthdata).

StatLink ⟨⟩ http://dx.doi.org/10.1787/550481682415

Definition and measurement

The World Health Organisation (WHO) defines low birth weight as a birth weight below 2 500 grams, irrespective of gestational age. This cut-off is based on epidemiological observations regarding the increased risk of death of the infant. The number of low birth weight births is then expressed as a percentage of total live births. The majority of the data comes from birth registers. However, data for the Netherlands and Turkey comes from a national health interview survey.

The infant mortality rate is the annual number of deaths of children under one year of age per 1 000 live births. Some international variation in infant mortality rates may be due to country variation in defining live children following birth. There are no gestational age or weight limits for birth mortality registration in Austria, Belgium, Denmark, Germany, Hungary, Italy, Portugal, the Slovak Republic, Finland, Spain, Sweden and the United Kingdom (EURO-PERISTAT Project 2008). There are also no limits in Canada and the United States. Minimal limits exist for Norway (to be counted as a death following birth the gestational age must exceed 12 weeks) and in the Czech Republic, France, the Netherlands and Poland a minimum gestational age of 22 weeks and/or a weight threshold of 500 g is applied. Australia and New Zealand have no gestational age limit. Requirements in the balance of OECD countries are unclear, but are not likely to differ greatly.

Low birth weight and infant mortality are both important indicators of infant health. Low birth weight infants have greater risks of poor health and development. Risk factors for both low birth weight and infant mortality include parental socio-economic status, maternal age, multiple births, maternal smoking and alcohol consumption, and timely access to and quality of pre-natal care.

On average across OECD countries 1 in every 15 children born is low birth weight. Iceland, Sweden, Finland and Korea reported the smallest proportions of low weight births among OECD countries, with 4.5% of low birth weight. Turkey, Japan and Greece are at the other end of the scale, with rates of low birth weight infants above 9% (HE3.1). Mexico, Hungary and the United States are close behind with over 8% of all live births reported as low birth weight.

On average one in 200 children born in the OECD dies in infancy. Infant mortality rates in OECD countries in 2006 ranged from lows of less than three deaths per 1 000 live births in Iceland, Sweden, Finland, Luxembourg and Japan, to highs of 18 and 23 deaths in Mexico and Turkey (HE3.2). Infant mortality rates were also relatively high in Poland, the Slovak Republic and the United States. All OECD countries have achieved remarkable progress in reducing infant mortality rates over the past four decades, with especially large falls in Portugal and Korea.

The prevalence of low birth weight infants has increased in several OECD countries in the last generation (HE3.3). There may be several reasons for this rise. First, the number of multiple births has risen steadily, partly as a result of the increase in fertility treatments. Second, women are increasingly delaying childbearing, which again implies an increase of the risk of low birth weight infants. Third, new medical technology and improved prenatal care are increasing survival of smaller infants.

Countries with a low proportion of low birth weight infants also have low infant mortality rates (HE3.4). Japan is an exception, with a highest proportion of low birth weight infants but a low infant mortality rate. Japan has recorded large rises in shares of low birth weight infants, rising from 5% of newborns in the late 1970s and approaching 10% by 2006. There are a number of possible causes. Smoking amongst younger Japanese women has increased and they are having their children at older ages (Jeong and Hurst, 2001).

Further reading

EURO-PERISTAT Project (2008), *European Perinatal Health Report*, *www.europeristat.com/publications/european-perinatal-health-report.shtml*.

Jeong, H.S. and J. Hurst (2001), "An Assessment of the Performance of the Japanese Health Care System", OECD Labour Market and Social Policy Occasional Papers, No. 56, OECD, Paris.

Figure notes

Figures HE3.1 and HE3.2: In Canada, Japan, the United States and some of the Nordic countries, very premature babies with a low chance of survival are registered as live births, resulting in higher reported rates compared to countries that do not.

Figure HE3.1: 2005 for Australia, Canada, Italy, Portugal and the United States. 2004 for Belgium, France and Sweden. 2003 for Luxembourg and Turkey.

Figure HE3.2: 2005 for Belgium, Canada and the United States. 2004 for Italy, 2002 for Korea.

HE3.1. On average across OECD countries, one in every 15 children born is low birth weight

Percentage of newborns weighing less than 2 500 g, 2006

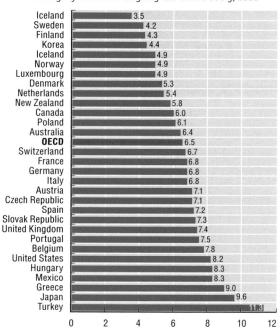

HE3.2. On average one in 200 children born in the OECD die in infancy

Deaths per 1 000 live births, 2006

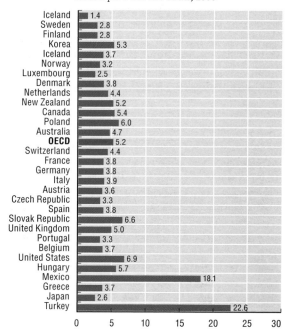

HE3.3. The prevalence of low birth weight infants has increased in several OECD countries in the last generation

Percentage of newborns weighing less than 2 500 g, 2006

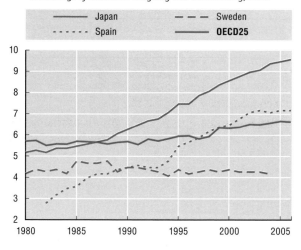

HE3.4. Countries with a small proportion of low birth weight infants also have low infant mortality

2006

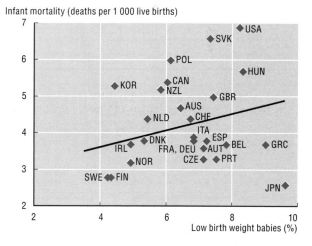

Source: OECD (2008), *OECD Health Data 2008*, OECD, Paris (*www.oecd.org/health/healthdata*).

StatLink ᐅᒲᔙ http://dx.doi.org/10.1787/550600314458

Definition and measurement

The most frequently used measure of being over-weight or obese is based on the body mass index (BMI). The BMI is defined as weight/height^2 (with weight in kilograms and height in metres). Adults with a BMI between 25 and 30 are defined as overweight, and those with a BMI over 30 as obese (WHO, 1997). This classification may not be suitable however for all ethnic groups, and adult thresholds are not suitable for children.

For most countries, estimates of overweight and obesity rates are based on self-reports of height and weight from health interview surveys. The exceptions are Australia, the Czech Republic, Luxembourg, New Zealand, the United Kingdom and the United States, where estimates are derived from actual measurement of height and weight. BMI estimates based on height and weight measurement are generally higher and more reliable than self-reports. For instance, in the United States, the adult obesity rate based on face-to-face interviews was 22% in 1999, compared with 31% in that same year based on actual measurements.

In many OECD countries, the growth in obesity has become a major public health concern. Obesity is a risk factor for hypertension, high cholesterol, diabetes, cardiovascular diseases, asthma, arthritis and some cancers. In the United States a study estimated that obesity costs exceed the *combined* costs of smoking and excessive drinking (Sturm, 2002). Health care costs attributed to obesity accounted for about 5-7% of total health spending in the United States in the late 1990s, and 2 to 3.5% of health spending in other countries like Canada, Australia and New Zealand (Thompson and Wolf, 2001). United States estimates indicate that the cost of health care services is 36% higher and the cost of medication 77% higher for obese people than for people of normal weight (Sturm, 2002).

There are many overweight and obese people in most OECD countries. Half or more of the adult population is now overweight or obese in Mexico, the United States, the United Kingdom, Australia, Greece, New Zealand, Luxembourg, Hungary, the Czech Republic, Canada, Germany, Portugal, Finland, Spain and Iceland. There are fewer overweight and obese people in OECD's two Asian countries (Japan and Korea) and in some European countries (France and Switzerland). Focussing only on obesity, which presents greater health risks than being overweight, the prevalence of obesity varies tenfold, from a low of 4% in Korea and Japan, to over 30% in the United States and Mexico (HE4.1).

Generally women are no more overweight and obese than men. However, in certain countries there are more overweight and obese men (Greece) whilst in others there are more overweight and obese women (Turkey, Mexico) (HE4.2).

More people are becoming overweight and obese. The rate of obesity has more than doubled over the past 20 years in the United States. It has almost tripled in Australia. It has more than tripled in the United Kingdom (HE4.3). Obesity rates in many western European countries have also increased substantially over the past decade.

More people are becoming overweight and obese across all population groups. But evidence from the United States, Canada and the United Kingdom indicates that overweight and obese people are more common among those in disadvantaged socio-economic groups, especially amongst women (Statistics Canada and Center for Disease Control and Prevention, 2004).

More children are also becoming overweight and obese. Child obesity rates are in double-figures in most OECD countries, with highs of one-third of children aged 13-14 in Spain (2000-02); 29% of children aged 5-17 in England (2004); and about one-fourth of children aged 5-17 in Italy (1993-2001) and 5-15 in Belgium (1998-99) (International Association for the Study of Obesity, 2007).

Further reading

Australian Institute of Health and Welfare (2004), *Australia's Health 2004*, AIHW Cat. No. AUS 44, Canberra.

International Association for the Study of Obesity (2007), "International Obesity Taskforce Database", available at *www.iotf.org/documents/Europeandatatable_000.pdf* (accessed on June 11, 2007).

Statistics Canada and Center for Disease Control and Prevention (2004), *Joint Canada/United States Survey of Health, 2002-2003*, Statistics Canada Cat. 82M0022-XIE, Ottawa.

Sturm, R. (2002), "The Effects of Obesity, Smoking and Drinking on Medical Problems and Costs", *Health Affairs*, Vol. 21, No. 2, pp. 245-253.

Thompson, D. and A.M. Wolf (2001), "The Medical-care Burden of Obesity", *Obesity Reviews*, Vol. 2, pp. 189-197.

World Health Organisation (1997), *Obesity: Preventing and Managing the Global Epidemic*, WHO, Geneva.

Figure note

Figures HE4.1 and HE4.2: Note 1: For Australia, the Czech Republic, Luxembourg, New Zealand, the United Kingdom and the United States, figures are based on actual height and weight measurement, rather than self-reports.

HE4.1. High obesity rates in many OECD countries

Percentage of adult population with BMI>30

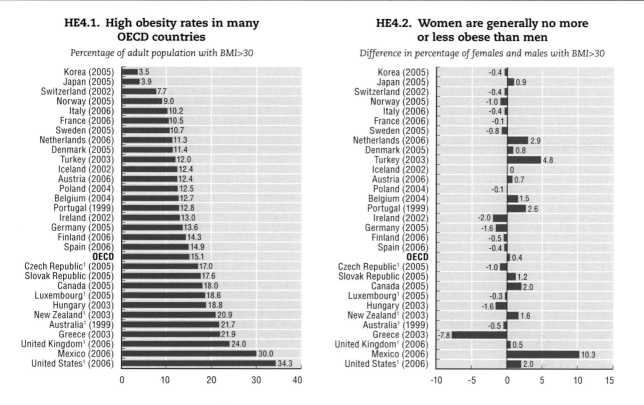

Country	%
Korea (2005)	3.5
Japan (2005)	3.9
Switzerland (2002)	7.7
Norway (2005)	9.0
Italy (2006)	10.2
France (2006)	10.5
Sweden (2005)	10.7
Netherlands (2006)	11.3
Denmark (2005)	11.4
Turkey (2003)	12.0
Iceland (2002)	12.4
Austria (2006)	12.4
Poland (2004)	12.5
Belgium (2004)	12.7
Portugal (1999)	12.8
Ireland (2002)	13.0
Germany (2005)	13.6
Finland (2006)	14.3
Spain (2006)	14.9
OECD	15.1
Czech Republic[1] (2005)	17.0
Slovak Republic (2005)	17.6
Canada (2005)	18.0
Luxembourg[1] (2005)	18.6
Hungary (2003)	18.8
New Zealand[1] (2003)	20.9
Australia[1] (1999)	21.7
Greece (2003)	21.9
United Kingdom[1] (2006)	24.0
Mexico (2006)	30.0
United States[1] (2006)	34.3

HE4.2. Women are generally no more or less obese than men

Difference in percentage of females and males with BMI>30

Korea (2005)	-0.4
Japan (2005)	0.9
Switzerland (2002)	-0.4
Norway (2005)	-1.0
Italy (2006)	-0.4
France (2006)	-0.1
Sweden (2005)	-0.8
Netherlands (2006)	2.9
Denmark (2005)	0.8
Turkey (2003)	4.8
Iceland (2002)	0
Austria (2006)	0.7
Poland (2004)	-0.1
Belgium (2004)	1.5
Portugal (1999)	2.6
Ireland (2002)	-2.0
Germany (2005)	-1.6
Finland (2006)	-0.5
Spain (2006)	-0.4
OECD	0.4
Czech Republic[1] (2005)	-1.0
Slovak Republic (2005)	1.2
Canada (2005)	2.0
Luxembourg[1] (2005)	-0.3
Hungary (2003)	-1.6
New Zealand[1] (2003)	1.6
Australia[1] (1999)	-0.5
Greece (2003)	-7.8
United Kingdom[1] (2006)	0.5
Mexico (2006)	10.3
United States[1] (2006)	2.0

HE4.3. Increasing obesity rates across the OECD

Percentage of adult population with a Body Mass Index over 30 over time, various years

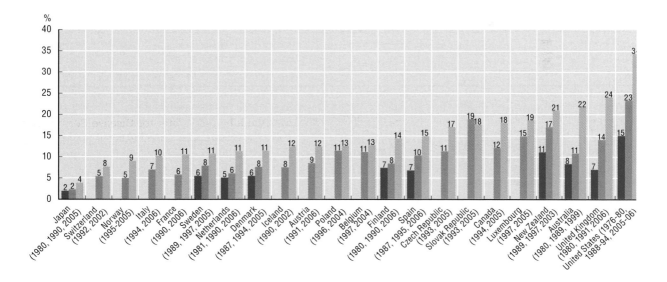

Source: OECD (2008), *OECD Health Data 2008*, CD-Rom, OECD, Paris (www.oecd.org/health/healthdata).

StatLink ⚙️ http://dx.doi.org/10.1787/550600403726

Definition and measurement

The height data focuses on people aged 20 to 49 years old. Below age 20, height growth may still occur and above age 50 people start physically shrinking. Measured height is preferred over self-reported height as evidence suggests that respondents tend to overestimate their own stature (Gorber *et al.*, 2007). This self-reporting bias varies according to age, sex, education, mode of interview, and purpose of the survey. Data from a recent systematic review suggests that unweighted average over-estimation of height from self reports by general adult male and female populations may be roughly about 1 cm in both cases (Gorber *et al.*, 2007). When height of age cohorts aged 20-24 years old is compared to that of those aged 45-49 years old to examine how recent adult height has been changing, some or all of this measurement error may be removed by the differencing. Where possible, data was obtained directly from specialised official health surveys.

Adult height is determined by a combination of genetic potential and net nutrition during childhood. Net nutrition is the quality and quantity of gross nutrition less losses due to physical activity and disease. Thus the environmental component of adult height is a cumulative summary of the child's dietary and disease environment (Steckel, 1995; Silventoinen, 2003). If the dietary and disease environment influences children with diminishing returns, country comparisons of average adult height also serve to indicate environmental inequality for children within the country.

Adult height varies considerably across the OECD. Males in the Nordic and Northern European countries are the tallest, in excess of 1.8 metres (HE5.1). The shortest men are found in Mexico, Portugal, Korea, and Japan, 10 cm or more shorter in height than in the tallest country. Figure HE5.1 also indicates similar country patterns for women, with the tallest women 1.68 metres and the shortest women 1.54 metres tall. The Nordic and Northern European height advantage may be in part due to effective healthcare and welfare systems. Of the shorter countries, Mexico has comparatively low income per head, while Japan and Korea compare more favourably to the rest of the OECD. There is little strong evidence that these country height differences are due to average country

differences in genetic endowments (Deaton, 2007). Overall, men are always taller than women. The ratio of male to female height ranges from 1.06 in Portugal to 1.09 in Australia, Mexico and the Netherlands. This sex difference does have a strong genetic component.

OECD countries are getting taller. Comparing the cohort aged 45-49 to the cohort aged 20-24 shows average OECD height rising by 3 cm for men and 2 cm for women over a 25 year period. This adult height gain indicates country improvements in childhood net nutrition. The star performer is Korea, where young men are 6 cm taller than their fathers' generation and women 4 cm taller than their mothers' generation. The poorest performer is the United States, where there have been no height gains over a generation (Komlos, 2008). Immigration of comparatively short people in recent times cannot explain height stagnation in the United States.

Short countries are catching up to taller countries. The scatter plots of Figure HE5.2 show that initially shorter Korean, Mexican, Spanish and Portuguese populations are increasing in height more rapidly than their taller Swedish, Icelandic, and Danish counterparts. Male height is converging faster than female height. For both men and women, the regression line showing convergence highlights the comparative under-performance of Mexico, Japan and the United States. The over-performers given their starting position on the height ladder are Korea, Spain and Ireland for men, and Korea, Spain and Belgium for women.

Further reading

Deaton, A. (2007), "Height, Health, and Development", *Proceedings of the National Academy of Sciences*, Vol. 104, pp. 13232-13237.

Gorber, S.C. *et al.* (2007), "A Comparison of Direct vs. Self-report Measures for Assessing Height, Weight, and BMI: A Systematic Review", *Obesity Reviews*, Vol. 8, No. 4, pp. 307-326.

Komlos, J. (2008), "Stagnation in Heights amongst Second-Generation U.S-born Army Personnel", *Social Science Quarterly*, Vol. 89, No. 2, pp. 445-455.

Silventoinen, K. (2003), "Determinants of Variation in Adult Height", *Journal of Biosocial Science*, Vol. 35, pp. 263-285.

Steckel, R. (1995), "Stature and the Standard of Living", *Journal of Economic Literature*, Vol. 33, No. 4, pp. 1903-1940.

Figure notes

Figure HE5.1: M = measured height, S = self-reported height and U = unknown method of height measurement.

HE5.1. Nordic and European countries are the tallest

Mean heights for men aged 20 to 49

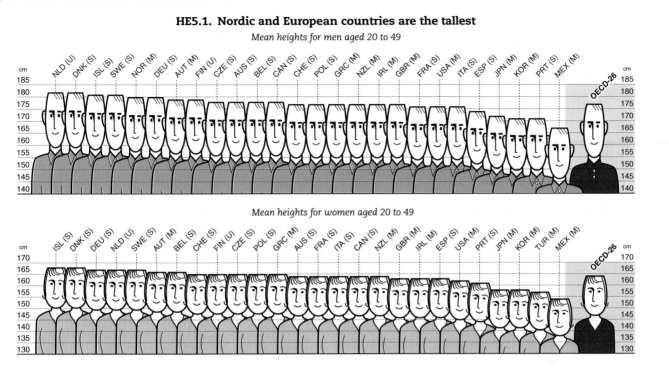

Mean heights for women aged 20 to 49

HE5.2. Male and female heights are converging towards those of the taller countries

Male convergence

Growth rate between the cohorts aged 45-49 years and 20-24 years, %

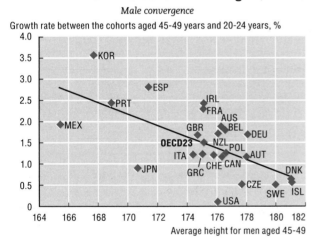

Average height for men aged 45-49

Female convergence

Growth rate between the cohorts aged 45-49 years and 20-24 years, %

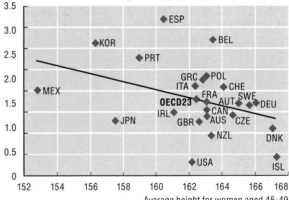

Average height for women aged 45-49

Source: Secretariat estimates and calculations from national and multinational health surveys (2001-07 where available).

StatLink 🔗 http://dx.doi.org/10.1787/550623158455

6. Mental health

Definition and measurement

The first data set used is from large-scale epidemiological surveys implemented as part of the World Health Organisation *World Mental Health Survey Initiative* (WMHSI). These surveys were conducted between 2002 and 2005 in ten OECD countries (three more OECD countries have surveys in the field). They use a common diagnostic instrument, the WHO Composite International Diagnostic instrument (CIDI), which measures the occurrence of various types of disorders, their nature and intensity, and the treatment provided.

Disorders considered include anxiety disorders, mood disorders; disorders linked to impulse control and disorders due to use of alcohol and drugs. All disorders are classified as serious, moderate, or mild.

The WMHSI data typically cover all people aged 18 and over. However the age limit is 16 years in New Zealand, 20 years in Japan, and 18-65 years in Mexico. Sample sizes range between around 2 000 (in the Netherlands) and 13 000 (New Zealand). Response rates vary between 50% (Belgium) and 80% (New Zealand). Survey samples are nationally representative in most countries, but they refer to all urban areas in Mexico and to four metropolitan areas in Japan. The European surveys do not assess bipolar disorders and substance abuse, seriously limiting comparability.

The second data set used is from the European Quality of Life Survey, European Foundation for the Improvement of Living and Working Conditions collected in late 2007. It covers a much larger number of member countries. It is, however, limited to Europe plus Turkey. The resulting index is based on self-reports to five questions, based on a short WHO index, picking up depressive-style symptoms.

Mental health disorders are a major burden on those who suffer them and on the public. The economic cost of mental health problems – including treatment and the indirect cost of lost productivity and days off work – are estimated at more than 2% of the GDP in the United Kingdom and slightly less in Canada (WHO, 2007).

Mental health problems are not uncommon. The share of people reporting having experienced any type of mental health disorder in the previous year ranged from 8% in Italy to 26% in the United States (HE6.1). More people report having incurred some mental health disorders during their lifetime, shares ranging from 18% in Italy and Japan, to around 40% or more in New Zealand and the United States.

In all countries, the most common disorders are due to anxiety, followed by mood disorders (HE6.2). Rarer are those due to impulse control and use of substances. A large part of all mental disorders are classified as mild, but 4% of the population of the countries covered report moderate disorders, and a further 3% report serious disorders – with a prevalence of serious disorders more than double this in the United States.

Most mental health disorders go untreated (HE6.3). While the proportion of treatment is higher on average for serious and moderate cases (at 48% and 31%, respectively), many serious cases receive no treatment.

A cross-21 country mental health index reveals relatively poor mental health in Turkey and good levels of mental health in Norway (HE6.3). Poor mental health is found to a lesser extent in Italy and Poland and good mental health to lesser extent in the Netherlands, Ireland and Germany. There is not a great deal of country variation through the middle of the mental health index.

Further reading

Kessler, R.C. *et al.* (2007), "Lifetime Prevalence and Age-of-Onset Distributions of Mental Disorders in the World Health Organisation World Mental Health Survey Initiative", *World Psychiatry*, Vol. 6, October.

OECD (2008), "Are All Jobs Good for Your health? The Impact of Work Status and Working Conditions on Mental Health", *OECD Employment Outlook*, OECD, Paris.

WHO World Mental Health Survey Consortium (2007), "Prevalence, Severity, and Unmet Need for Treatment of Mental Disorders in the World Health Organisation World Mental Health Surveys", *American Medical Association*, Vol. 291, No. 21, June.

HE6.1. Annual and life-time prevalence of mental health problems in ten OECD countries

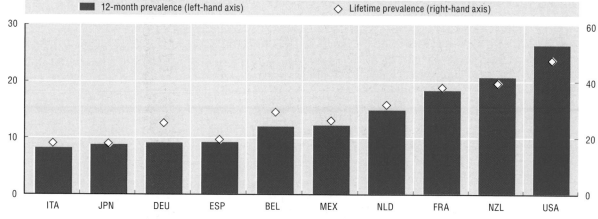

Source: WHO World Mental Health Survey Consortium (2007).

HE6.2. Type, severity and treatment of mental health problems in ten OECD countries

	12-month prevalence, percentage share of total population								Share mental health disorders receiving treatment				
	By type					By severity			By severity				
	Anxiety	Mood	Impulse-control	Substance	Any disorder	Serious	Moderate	Mild	Serious	Moderate	Mild	None	Total
Belgium	7	6	1	1	12	2	3	6	54	50	28	7	11
France	12	9	1	1	18	3	6	10	63	36	22	8	12
Germany	6	4	0	1	9	1	3	5	50	31	28	5	8
Italy	6	4	0	0	8	1	3	4	..	31	19	2	5
Japan	5	3	1	2	9	2	4	3	..	17	11	5	6
Mexico	7	5	1	3	12	4	4	5	20	19	10	3	4
Netherlands	9	7	1	3	15	2	4	9	50	35	27	7	11
New Zealand	15	8	1	4	23	0	0	0	..	..	..	..	..
Spain	6	5	1	0	9	1	3	5	65	38	35	4	7
United States	18	10	7	4	26	8	9	9	52	34	23	8	15
Average	9	6	2	2	15	3	4	6	48	31	21	6	9

Source: WHO World Mental Health Survey Consortium (2007).

HE6.3. Mental health index for 21 European OECD countries
Percentage, 2007, higher value is better mental health

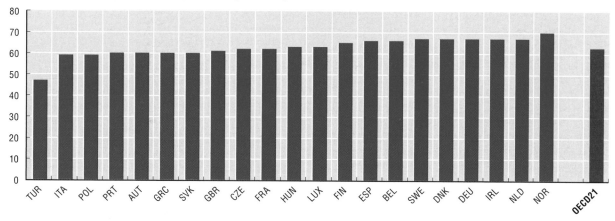

Source: Second European Quality of Life Survey, European
Foundation for the Improvement of Living and Working Conditions,
2007, www.eurofound.europa.eu/publications/htmlfiles/ef0852.htm.

StatLink  http://dx.doi.org/10.1787/550627528424

Definition and measurement

Long-term care recipients are those receiving formal paid care for an extended period of time due to issues of functional physical or cognitive capacity. Recipients are dependent on help with activities such as bathing, dressing, eating, getting into and out of bed or chair, moving around and using the bathroom. Help is frequently provided in combination with basic medical services. Long-term care can be received in an institution or at home.

The international data comparability is limited. Data generally refer to a specific day in the year but to a week for Denmark, a month for Japan and the entire year for Hungary and New Zealand and for home care recipients in the Czech Republic and Switzerland. For the Czech Republic, Italy and the Slovak Republic, data are available for recipients of all ages. In Austria, Belgium and Poland, the elderly age threshold is 60 (instead of 65), while it is 67 (instead of 65) in Norway and 75 (instead of 80) in Poland. Third, data include privately-funded care recipients in some countries (the Czech Republic, Finland, Germany, Ireland, Poland, Switzerland, the United Kingdom and the United States).

Long-term care systems vary tremendously across OECD countries. Nordic countries have extensive long-term care systems. The share of recipients in these countries was more than 15% of those over age 65 in 2006 (HE7.1). Other countries with universal and comprehensive long-term care coverage (e.g., Austria, Germany, Japan, Luxembourg and the Netherlands) also have a relatively high recipients share. On the other hand, in Korea, Italy and Eastern European countries (except Hungary), where formal arrangements for long-term care are not widespread, the share of those over age 65 receiving long-term care is between 0.6% and 3.6%.

There is convergence in proportions of old people in long-term care. The share of total long-term care recipients increased in countries with a relatively low share around 2000 (Australia, Belgium, Iceland, Italy, Japan and Korea). On the other hand, it declined in countries which had a share above the OECD average in 2000 (Finland, Germany, Norway, Sweden and Switzerland), as well as in Ireland and the United States.

Home care arrangements predominate in most OECD countries. A shift from institutional to home care can be observed in Australia, Belgium, Italy, Japan, Korea and Sweden. This shift reflects both older people's preferences and an attempt to reduce reliance on expensive institutional care (OECD, 2005). Germany, however, experienced a recent shift in the opposite direction (Gibson and Redfoot, 2007).

The "older" old are much more likely to be in long-term care. Among the oldest age cohort (80 and over), the average OECD share of long-term care recipients is over five times higher than the proportion of recipients aged between 65-79. The share of recipients in the 80 years and over cohort has been shrinking in most countries except for Australia, Iceland and Japan (HE5.2). A similar declining recipient proportion is occurring for the 65-79 year-old age cohort.

More women than men are long-term care recipients. The average recipient share of the 65-79 year-old female population is over a third higher than the male share. This gap becomes greater among the over 80-year-old recipients, where the average share of female recipients is one and a half times the male share (HE5.3). This over-representation is consistent with a higher prevalence of disability among elderly women (Lafortune et al., 2007).

Further reading

Gibson, M.J. and Redfoot, D.L. (2007), *Comparing Long-Term Care in Germany and the United States: What Can We Learn From Each Other?*, AARP, Washington, DC.

Lafortune, G. et al. (2007), "Trends in Severe Disability Among Elderly People: Assessing the Evidence in 12 OECD Countries and the Future Implications", OECD Health Working Papers No. 26, OECD, Paris.

OECD (2005), *Long-term Care for Older People*, OECD, Paris.

Figure notes

Figures HE7.1 to HE7.3: Data on home care recipients are not available for Canada, Iceland, Ireland, the Slovak Republic and the United States, and for HE7.1, data on home care recipients are not available for Switzerland. Data on people receiving care in institutions refer to 1999 (the United States) and 2001 (Ireland) instead of 2000, and 2003 (Canada) and 2004 (the United States) instead of 2006. Data on both institutional and home care recipients refer to 2001 (United Kingdom) and 2002 (Australia and Japan) instead of 2000, and 2003 (Austria, France and the Slovak Republic), 2004 (Belgium, Korea and the United Kingdom) and 2005 (Australia and Switzerland) instead of 2006. For other data specifications, refer to the information available in the Statlink. Note 1 : Data refer to different age-breakdowns. For France, data on home care recipients refer to recipients aged 60 and over while data on recipients in institutions refer to recipients aged 65 and over. Corresponding population data are used to calculate the share except Norway, for which people aged 65 and over (instead of 67 and over) are used to calculate the share, resulting in underestimation. Note 2: Data do not refer to a specific day in the year, resulting in overestimation. Note 3: Data include care recipients who are fully paying their care from private sources. For the Czech Republic, only data on home care include privately-funded recipients.

HE7.1. Most formal long-term care recipients receive care at home

People aged 65 and over living in institutions and receiving formal care at home as a share of people aged 65 and over, 2000 and 2006

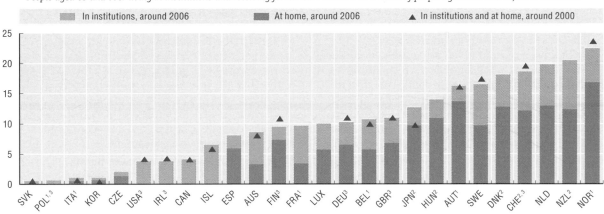

HE7.2. The proportion of formal long-term care recipients is higher at older age groups but has decreased since 2000 in many OECD countries

Recipients aged between 65 and 79 and aged 80 and over, as a share of the respective age group population, 2000 and 2006

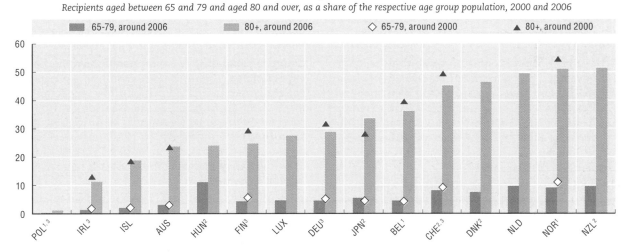

HE7.3. A larger share of elderly women receive formal long-term care than men

Female and male recipients aged between 65 and 79 and 80 and over, as a share of respective age group and male/female population, 2006

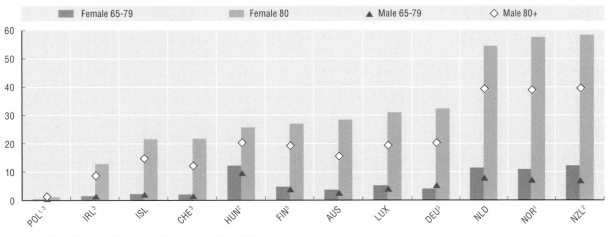

Source: OECD (2008), *OECD Health Data 2008*, OECD, Paris (www.oecd.org/health/healthdata) and OECD Demographic and Labour Force database.

StatLink 🔗 http://dx.doi.org/10.1787/550628454651

8. Health care expenditure

Definition and measurement

Total expenditure on health measures the final consumption of health goods and services plus capital investment in health care infrastructure. It includes both public and private spending on personal health care, and collective health services (public health and prevention programmes and administration). Excluded are health-related expenditures such as training, research and environmental health.

To compare health care expenditures across countries and time, health expenditure per capita is deflated by a national price index and converted to US dollars using purchasing power parity (PPP) exchange rates.

Average per capita health spending varies considerably across OECD countries. In 2006, the highest spending OECD country is the United States, devoting USD 6 714 per capita to health – more than twice the OECD average. After the United States come Norway, Switzerland and Luxembourg, all still well above the OECD average. Most OECD countries are clustered in a band between USD 2 400 and USD 3 600. At the other end of the scale a group of four countries (Turkey, Mexico, Poland, and the Slovak Republic), spends less than half the OECD average.

Variation in the levels of public health spending is similar to that observed for total health spending. Figure HE8.1 also shows the United States as the highest proportional health spender, by a considerable margin over Portugal, with Turkey the lowest spender.

A rising share of resources is being devoted to health. Between 1995 and 2006, average OECD health expenditure per capita has grown annually by around 4% (HE8.2). Average economic growth over the same period was 2.5%. However, behind this OECD average, significant variations can be observed both between countries and over time. In general, the high growth countries, such as Korea and Ireland, have been those that started out with relatively lower health expenditures per capita. Health expenditure growth in these two countries has greatly exceeded the OECD average over this period. By contrast, countries such as Germany and Austria have experienced relatively moderate health expenditure growth between 1995 and 2006, partly as a result of cost-containment measures and slow economic growth.

Richer countries spend more on health. Figure HE8.3 shows a positive association between average income and health expenditure per capita across OECD countries. Country income is not the sole factor influencing health expenditure levels. The association tends to be stronger among OECD countries with lower average income. For countries with similar average income levels there are substantial differences in health expenditure. For example, despite Japan and Germany having similar average income levels, their health spending per capita differs considerably.

Countries spending more on health have higher life expectancies. Higher health spending per capita is generally associated with higher life expectancy at birth (HE8.4), although this relationship is less pronounced amongst countries with higher health spending per capita. Given their levels of health spending, Japan stands out as having relatively high life expectancy and the United States has relatively low life expectancy.

Figure notes

Figure HE8.1: Belgium and Denmark: Public and private expenditures exclude capital expenditures. Note 1: 2005/06. Note 2: 2005.

Figure HE8.2: Note 1: Series breaks. Note 2: 1999-2005. Note 3: 1997-2005. Note 4: 1995-2005.

HE8.1. Health spending as a share of NNI, 2006

Countries ranked by health spending as a share of NNI

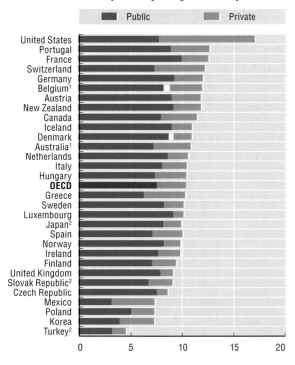

Legend: Public | Private

Countries (top to bottom): United States, Portugal, France, Switzerland, Germany, Belgium[1], Austria, New Zealand, Canada, Iceland, Denmark, Australia[1], Netherlands, Italy, Hungary, **OECD**, Greece, Sweden, Luxembourg, Japan[2], Spain, Norway, Ireland, Finland, United Kingdom, Slovak Republic[2], Czech Republic, Mexico, Poland, Korea, Turkey[2]

HE8.2. Annual growth in per capita health spending, 1995-2006

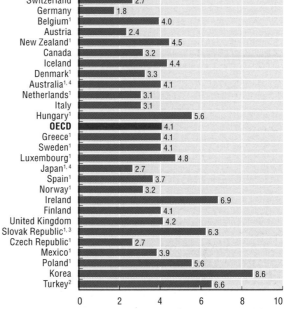

United States	3.4
Portugal[1]	4.2
France[1]	2.7
Switzerland	2.7
Germany	1.8
Belgium[1]	4.0
Austria	2.4
New Zealand[1]	4.5
Canada	3.2
Iceland	4.4
Denmark[1]	3.3
Australia[1,4]	4.1
Netherlands[1]	3.1
Italy	3.1
Hungary[1]	5.6
OECD	4.1
Greece[1]	4.1
Sweden[1]	4.1
Luxembourg[1]	4.8
Japan[1,4]	2.7
Spain[1]	3.7
Norway[1]	3.2
Ireland	6.9
Finland	4.1
United Kingdom	4.2
Slovak Republic[1,3]	6.3
Czech Republic[1]	2.7
Mexico[1]	3.9
Poland[1]	5.6
Korea	8.6
Turkey[2]	6.6

HE8.3. Richer countries spend more per capita on health care, 2006

Health expenditure per capita (USD, PPP), 2006

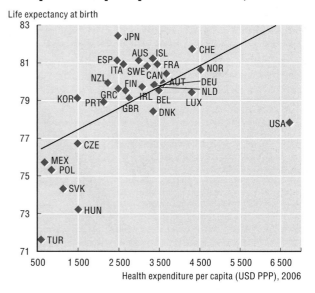

NNI per capita (USD, PPP), 2006

HE8.4. Countries with higher life expectancy spend more per capita on health care, 2006

Life expectancy at birth

Health expenditure per capita (USD PPP), 2006

Source: OECD (2008), *OECD Health Data 2008*, OECD, Paris
(*www.oecd.org/health/healthdata*).

StatLink http://dx.doi.org/10.1787/550650860842

8. SOCIAL COHESION INDICATORS

1. Life satisfaction

2. Work satisfaction

3. Crime victimisation

4. Suicides

5. Bullying

6. Risky behaviour

Definition and measurement

The main indicator of life satisfaction used is from the Gallup World Poll 2006. The Gallup World Poll was based on nationally representative samples of people aged 15 years and older. It uses the same questionnaire in all countries, ensuring maximum comparability, although there are issues about the extent to which the English-language concept of "life satisfaction" is translatable into the different languages used across the OECD. However, the problem is less than for happiness-style questions, which is why life-satisfaction questions are used here

The Gallup World Poll ask respondents to "imagine an eleven-rung ladder where the bottom (0) represents the worst possible life for you and the top (10) represents the best possible life for you. On which step of the ladder do you feel you personally stand at the present time?". The main indicator used in this section is the average country score.

Access to detailed Gallup World Poll data by socio-demographic characteristics was not possible. There are questions about data reliability from land-line, phone-based interviews like Gallup in countries where mobile phone coverage is high. In terms of consideration of changes in life satisfaction, data came from the World Happiness Data base from a variety of sources, primarily the *Eurobarometer* survey and *World Values Survey* (see Box 1.1 in Chapter 1 for more detail).

There are considerable differences between countries regarding the degree to which people are satisfied with their lives (CO1.1). Denmark, Switzerland and Finland, the three countries with the highest life satisfaction, are 2.7 average steps higher up the 11-step ladder compared with the bottom three countries (the Slovak Republic, Italy and Turkey).

There are broad regional or cultural country groupings of life satisfaction. Three of the top six countries are Nordic, with Iceland a Nordic outlier in the middle of the pack. Continental western and eastern European OECD members are not particularly satisfied with their lives, with the notable exceptions of the Swiss and the Dutch and, to a lesser extent, the Belgians and Spanish. Predominantly Anglophone OECD countries (United Kingdom, Ireland, the United States, New Zealand, Australia and Canada) are all in the top half of life satisfaction, and follow in a tight group after the largely Nordic top cluster.

Life satisfaction is higher in richer OECD countries (CO1.2). The relationship is strong. But it also appears to be non-linear. This non-linearity may indicate that increments in income add less to life satisfaction as countries become richer. There are interesting outliers from the regression line. Mexico, New Zealand and Denmark all generate considerably higher amounts of life satisfaction than predicted, whilst Luxembourg, Ireland and Turkey all generate much lower life satisfaction than predicted by their NNI.

Countries which achieve high satisfaction also share it more equally across their population (CO1.3). Lower country average life satisfaction is associated with greater inequality of life satisfaction within that country, as measured by the standard deviation of individual scores. The relationship is a strong one.

Life satisfaction is improving over time. Figure CO1.4 shows that average OECD life satisfaction has improved by an average 0.28 steps on the 11-step ladder. Life satisfaction rose or remained constant in 23 countries and only declined in Portugal, Hungary, the United States, Canada and Japan. The rise in life satisfaction in Turkey is particularly striking.

Further reading

Deaton, A. (2007), "Income, Aging, Health and Wellbeing around the World: Evidence from the Gallup World Poll", NBER Working Paper No. 13317, Cambridge, MA.

Figure note

Figure CO1.4: In most cases the life-satisfaction change data covers the six-year period 2000-06. For the sources and country exceptions, see Box 1.1 in Chapter 1.

CO1.1. Considerable differences between countries regarding life satisfaction

Average points of life satisfaction on an 11-step ladder from 0-10, 2006

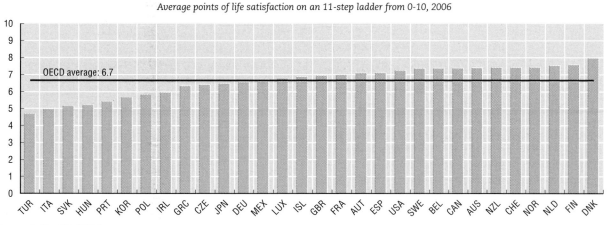

Source: Gallup World Poll.

CO1.2. Life satisfaction rises with higher NNI, 2006

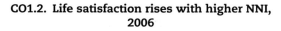

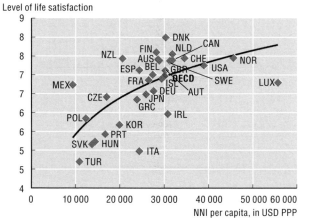

CO1.3. Lower life satisfaction is associated with greater inequality of life satisfaction, 2006

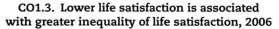

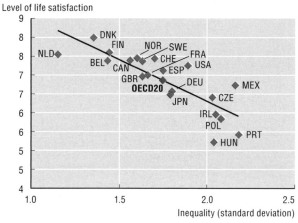

Source: Gallup World Poll; OECD National Accounts (www.oecd.org/statistics/national-accounts).

CO1.4. Life satisfaction is rising in most OECD countries

Changes in life satisfaction, points on an 11-step ladder, 2000-06

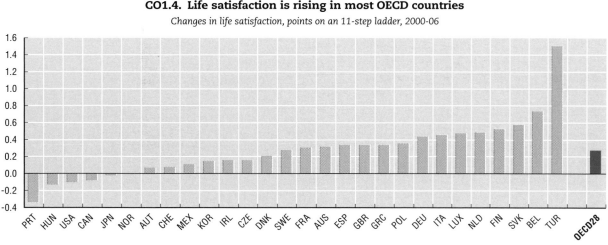

Source: World Happiness database (http://worlddatabaseofhappiness.eur.nl).   StatLink ⬛🖳 http://dx.doi.org/10.1787/550664800231

Definition and measurement

Measures of work satisfaction are taken from Wave III of the *International Social Science Programme*. The last Work Orientation wave of ISSP was in 2005. Previous waves were conducted in 1989 and 1997. The survey is addressed to people aged 16 and over working either as an employee or as a self-employed. 21 OECD countries participated in the latest wave of this survey. The survey has high and variable rates of non-response between countries and over time, as well as different country sampling frames, all of which may undermine comparability.

The basic indicator of work satisfaction used here is to the share of all employees reporting that they felt "completely", "very" or "fairly" satisfied in their main job (out of seven response categories). Also shown are measures of job values and job outcomes reported by respondents. Job values are based on questions that ask "for you personally, how important" are a range of factors (with six response categories). Similarly, job outcomes are based on questions that ask whether respondents agree or disagree to different statements about their current job (always with six response categories). In both cases, the questions posed imply no ranking among categories. Sample sizes are small, between around 1000 and 2000. Data for Belgium are limited to Flanders, those for Germany to the western *Länder*, and those for the United Kingdom exclude Northern Ireland.

Most people are satisfied with their jobs (CO2.1). On average across 21 OECD countries, the share of people reporting to be completely, very or fairly satisfied with their jobs was close to 80%. Figures ranged from around 70% in Korea to more than 90% in Mexico and Switzerland. Around 12% of respondents were completely satisfied, on average, as compared to 30% being very satisfied, and to 40% being fairly satisfied.

More people are becoming satisfied with their jobs. Since 1997, in the 11 OECD countries where comparison is possible, the share of employees satisfied has improved by around 5 points. Large rises are found in Sweden while falls occur in France, Spain and Denmark (CO2.1).

There is little difference in job satisfaction by gender and age. Across the 21 OECD countries covered in the 2005 survey, women were as satisfied with work as men. Women reported lower job satisfaction than men in Portugal, Switzerland, Belgium, Korea, Germany, Japan and the United States, and higher job satisfaction in Ireland, the Czech Republic, Australia, Mexico and Finland. Job satisfaction increases slightly with age until 65, although there are several country exceptions (ISSP 2005).

Job security is the attribute most valued by workers. Next come high income, opportunities for advancements and working time flexibility, although with large quantitative differences across countries (ISSP 2005).

Most people are happy with their current combination of hours and pay. When asked whether they would prefer to work the same number of hours for the same money, more hours for more money, or fewer hours for less money, a majority in all countries were satisfied with the same number of hours and money. Around a third of respondents wanted to work more hours for more money. Up to half or more in Mexico and France wanted more hours and more money. In Denmark, however, there are more people wanting shorter hours/less money than wanting longer hours/more money. Differences between the two groups preferring change are also negligible in other Nordic countries and Switzerland (ISSP 2005).

Further reading

International Social Survey Programme (ISSP) (2005), Work Orientations III, Data and Documentation, *www.gesis.org/en/services/data/survey-data/issp/modules-study-overview/work-orientations/2005/*.

Vecernik, J. (2003), "Skating on Thin Ice: A Comparison of Work Values and Job Satisfaction in CEE and EU Countries", *International Journal of Comparative Sociology*, Vol. 44, pp. 444-471, December.

Figure and table notes

Figure CO2.1: Countries are ranked, from left to right, in increasing order of share of people satisfied in their jobs.

Table CO2.2: These data are based on selected outcomes, not a coding of open ended responses.

CO2.1. High and rising: work satisfaction across the OECD

Percentage of all employees completely, very or fairly satisfied with their job, 2005

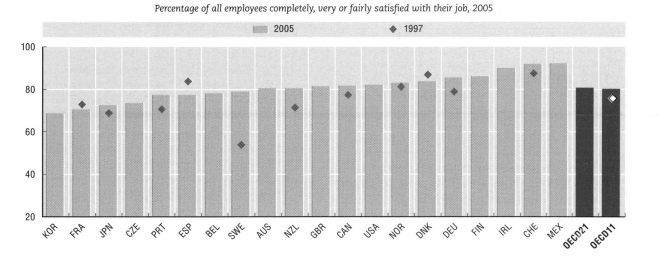

CO2.2. Job attributes and job characteristics most valued by respondents, 2005

	Important attributes of all jobs				Characteristics of the job held by respondents							Preferences on working time	
								Hard work					
	Job security	High income	Opportunities for advancement	Decide time of work	Job security	High income	Opportunities for advancement	Come home from work exhausted	Hard physical work	Stressful work	Dangerous conditions	Prefer to spend less time on the job	Prefer to spend more time on the job
Australia	95	71	83	55	64	24	25	90	45	85	29	67	33
Belgium	96	80	81	64	65	23	26	80	45	81	34	69	31
Canada	91	82	82	60	64	34	31	86	40	85	29	78	22
Czech Republic	94	86	57	54	51	17	14	88	48	62	32	78	22
Denmark	81	59	41	61	74	41	23	87	48	81	29	82	18
Finland	94	82	47	72	60	30	20	84	47	84	36	72	28
France	92	82	77	57	51	13	12	92	52	87	33	61	39
Germany	96	77	76	54	71	25	23	86	46	81	28	39	61
Hungary	99	93	67	47	55	15	15	94	59	71	47	31	69
Ireland	94	79	88	58	75	33	36	82	42	66	25	62	38
Japan	85	78	27	52	61	24	10	74	43	72	25	74	26
Korea	97	93	91	68	40	16	25	83	69	87	39	21	79
Mexico	98	92	97	79	71	26	44	80	47	60	32	16	84
New Zealand	93	70	83	61	68	30	31	84	48	78	33	71	29
Norway	93	70	52	61	62	18	13	86	42	86	33	67	33
Portugal	97	93	93	69	62	16	36	88	49	73	29	47	53
Spain	97	95	88	78	69	26	24	79	51	72	37	63	37
Sweden	93	74	49	70	65	19	21	86	51	89	33	83	17
Switzerland	93	60	65	69	68	32	34	82	40	76	25	60	40
United Kingdom	95	74	78	54	68	20	27	90	51	86	24	72	28
United States	93	81	88	53	74	27	38	85	47	79	32	54	46
OECD21	**94**	**80**	**72**	**62**	**64**	**24**	**25**	**85**	**48**	**78**	**32**	**60**	**40**

Source: ISSP Work Orientation, wave III (2005).

StatLink 〰️🔧 http://dx.doi.org/10.1787/550708264007

Definition and measurement

Crime comparisons between countries can be made via surveys designed to assess experience with actual criminal victimisation. Crime statistics shown here are based on the 2005 *International Crime Victim Survey*, run by a consortium coordinated by the United Nations Interregional Criminal Justice Research Institute (UNICRI) and the United Nation Office on Drugs and Crime (UNODC). ICVS data for European countries are drawn from the *European Survey on Crime and Safety*, organised by a consortium led by Gallup Europe (see *www.europeansafetyobservatory.eu/euics_rp.htm for detail*). Data drawn on for changes is from a variety of years.

The ICVS focuses on ten types of "conventional" crimes (the distinction is that of the ICVS). Respondents are asked about victimisation by these conventional crimes that they themselves or their households experienced. These crimes cover vehicle-related crimes (theft of a car, from or out of a car, of a bicycle and motorcycle), burglary (completed and attempted), theft of personal property, and contact crimes (robbery, sexual offences – reported only for women, and assault or threat). Also covered are drug-related problems and "non-conventional" crimes such as, hate crime, street level corruption and consumer fraud (including internet-based fraud and credit card theft). The ICVS also provides information on reactions to crime, fears of crime, and use of preventive measures. While survey results are based on nationally representative samples, results are affected by design features such as mode of interviewing and period of fieldwork. Sample sizes are usually small (2000 people in most countries). Comparability problems and variable under-reporting may exist for crimes of intimate partner violence or of a sexual nature. Equally, people may experience crimes like fraud and corruption but may not realise it, again leading to under-reporting.

One person in six in the OECD countries was a victim of a conventional crime (CO3.1). In 2004-05 victimisation exceeded 20% in Ireland, New Zealand, Iceland and the United Kingdom. Conversely, victimisation rates are below 10% in Japan and Spain.

Victimisation rates have declined in the new millennium, at least for the ten categories of conventional crime. There have been falls in 18 out of the 20 OECD countries for which information is available. The fall in the victimisation rate exceeds 5 points in Spain, Italy, Australia, Sweden and France. Small rises are recorded in Switzerland and Norway.

Less severe crimes are the most frequent (CO3.2). On average, across all OECD countries included in Table CO3.2, 3.7% of the population reported having experienced theft of personal property and pickpocketing – with much higher levels in Ireland and much lower ones in Japan – while 3.1% reported bicycle theft and 2.9% experienced assaults or threats.

Being a victim of a crime involving direct personal contact is comparatively rare. The share of assault or threat victims ranges from around 5% or more in Iceland, Ireland and New Zealand, to less than 1% in Japan, Italy and Portugal. On average, around 1% of the population declared having been victim of a robbery, with much higher levels in Mexico and Ireland. Sexual offences against women are reported by around 1.8% of female respondents, and by 3% or more in Ireland, the United States, Sweden and Iceland.

Unexpectedly, non-conventional crimes are more common than conventional ones. On average, 11% of respondents declare having experienced some types of consumer fraud for example, ranging from close to 25% in Greece to less than 2% in Japan. The share of people reporting a personal experience of corruption is small on average, but much higher in Greece and Mexico than elsewhere in the OECD.

Further reading

Van Djik J., J. Van Kesteren and P. Smit Paul (2008), "Criminal Victimisation in International Perspective – Key Findings from the 2004-2005 International Crime Victims Survey and European Survey on Crime and Safety", WODC Publication No. 257, January.

Figure and table notes

Figure CO3.1: Note 1: 1996 for Austria, 1992 for Italy and New Zealand, and 1989 for Norway, Germany and Spain.

Table CO3.2: Sexual offences against women are rates for the female population only.

CO3.1. Conventional crime is falling across the OECD, 2000 to 2004-05
Percentage of people reporting at least one of the ten categories over the previous 12 months

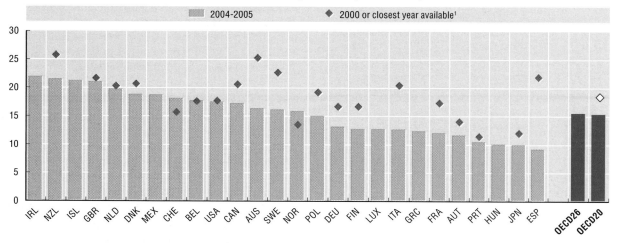

CO3.2. Experience of different types of crimes and fear of crime
Percentage of people reporting experience over the previous 12 months, 2004-05

	All conventional victimisation	Vehicle-related crimes				Burglary and other thefts			Contact crimes			Non-conventional crimes		Fears of crime
		Theft of cars	Theft from or out of cars	Motor-cycle theft	Bicycle theft	Burglary with entry	Attempted burglary	Theft of personal property and pick-pocketing	Robbery	Sexual offences against women	Assaults or threats	Consumer fraud	Corruption	Feeling unsafe or very unsafe on the street after dark
Australia	16.3	1.1	4.5	0.1	1.2	2.5	2.4	3.6	0.9	..	3.4	..	..	27.0
Austria	11.6	0.1	2.4	0.0	2.0	0.9	1.4	3.4	0.4	2.2	1.8	8.1	0.6	19.0
Belgium	17.7	0.5	4.2	0.1	4.2	1.8	2.4	3.4	1.2	0.9	3.6	8.0	0.5	26.0
Canada	17.2	0.8	4.8	0.2	2.7	2.0	1.7	4.0	0.8	2.3	3.0	7.4	0.6	17.0
Denmark	18.8	1.3	2.6	0.3	6.0	2.7	1.6	3.3	0.9	1.9	3.3	15.7	1.0	17.0
Finland	12.7	0.4	2.2	0.1	5.2	0.8	0.5	2.3	0.3	1.4	2.2	5.2	0.0	14.0
France	12.0	0.6	3.2	0.3	0.9	1.6	1.2	3.3	0.8	0.4	2.1	10.2	1.1	21.0
Germany	13.1	0.2	2.0	0.2	3.4	0.9	1.3	3.0	0.4	2.4	2.7	11.7	0.6	30.0
Greece	12.3	0.3	1.8	0.6	2.1	1.8	1.7	5.3	1.4	1.7	2.4	24.7	13.5	42.0
Hungary	10.0	0.2	2.1	0.0	1.7	1.7	0.8	3.0	0.9	0.1	1.2	19.7	4.9	26.0
Iceland	21.2	1.0	3.8	0.1	4.6	1.6	1.6	6.9	0.8	3.0	5.9	12.9	0.3	6.0
Ireland	21.9	1.2	5.2	0.3	2.5	2.3	1.7	7.2	2.2	3.8	4.9	8.0	0.3	27.0
Italy	12.6	1.0	2.4	1.0	2.1	2.1	2.5	2.4	0.3	0.7	0.8	5.9	0.4	35.0
Japan	9.9	0.1	1.1	0.7	5.1	0.9	0.7	0.3	0.2	1.3	0.6	1.9	0.2	35.0
Luxembourg	12.7	0.6	2.8	0.0	1.6	1.7	2.7	2.9	0.7	0.6	2.3	9.8	0.4	36.0
Mexico	18.7	0.9	4.1	0.0	3.7	3.0	3.0	4.3	3.0	1.5	2.2	7.2	13.3	34.0
Netherlands	19.7	1.0	3.9	0.4	6.6	1.3	1.4	3.7	0.5	1.9	4.3	7.0	0.2	18.0
New Zealand	21.5	1.8	6.6	0.1	1.4	3.2	3.1	4.1	1.1	2.5	4.9	7.7	0.5	30.0
Norway	15.8	0.7	2.6	0.3	4.2	1.2	0.9	4.8	0.8	2.5	2.9	9.7	0.4	14.0
Poland	15.0	0.7	3.9	0.1	2.6	1.4	1.1	3.5	1.3	1.3	3.0	16.1	4.4	33.0
Portugal	10.4	1.5	5.0	0.0	0.5	1.4	0.8	1.6	1.0	0.5	0.9	8.2	1.0	34.0
Spain	9.1	1.0	2.7	0.3	0.7	0.8	0.4	2.1	1.3	0.3	1.6	10.8	0.3	33.0
Sweden	16.1	0.5	4.2	0.6	5.0	0.7	0.1	2.4	1.1	3.3	3.5	13.7	0.1	19.0
Switzerland	18.1	0.2	2.9	0.6	4.6	1.6	1.2	5.9	0.8	2.9	2.5	7.3	0.5	..
United Kingdom	21.0	1.8	5.8	0.7	2.7	3.3	2.6	5.7	1.3	1.9	5.4	..	..	31.0
United States	17.5	1.1	5.2	0.0	2.9	2.5	2.6	4.8	0.6	3.6	4.3	12.5	0.5	19.0
OECD26	**15.5**	**0.8**	**3.5**	**0.3**	**3.1**	**1.8**	**1.6**	**3.7**	**1.0**	**1.8**	**2.9**	**10.4**	**1.9**	**25.7**

Source: Van Djik J., J. Van Kesteren and P. Smit Paul (2008), "Criminal Victimisation in International Perspective – Key Findings from the 2004-2005 International Crime Victims Survey and European Survey on Crime and Safety", WODC Publication No. 257, January.

StatLink ⌐ⅅⅅ http://dx.doi.org/10.1787/550717741440

Definitions and measurement

Data on suicide rates are based on official regis-ters on causes of death. They are standardised using the OECD population structure of 1980, accounting for changes in the age structure across countries and over time. Suicide rates are expressed in deaths per 100 000 individuals.

Countries have different procedures for recording suicide as the underlying cause of death, despite the development of the International Statistical Classification of Diseases and Related Health Problems (ICD), and procedures may have changed over time. In addition suicide may be under-reported because of a societal stigma attached to suicide. This socio-cultural norm may vary across countries and over time.

Studies assessing the reliability of suicide statis-tics suggest that sources of error are random. Thus there is little impact on comparing rates between countries, between demographic groups or over time (Sainsbury and Jenkins, 1982).

Suicide rates increased in the 1970s and peaked at the beginning of the 1980s (CO4.1). While most coun-tries' suicide rates follow this broad pattern, Japan, Korea and Ireland do not share it. In Japan, suicide rates are lower than in 1960, but have remained at relatively high levels (around 20 deaths per 100 000 persons) since 1997. Suicides in Korea show a sharp increase from the late 1990s. Korea now has the highest suicide rates among OECD countries (around 22 deaths per 100 000 individuals). Ireland shows a marked regular increase of suicide rates with a peak in 2000, followed by a small but continuous decline.

Suicide rates have fallen for men and women and the gender gap has been fairly stable. Because both male and female rates have fallen similarly, gender gaps remain at similar levels and suicide continues to be a predominantly male phenomenon. On average, for each female suicide there are about three male deaths. Yet there are marked variations across countries in gender gaps (CO4.2). Larger differences prevail in Mexico, Poland and the Slovak Republic, where for each female death there are at least five male deaths. By contrast, in Korea, the Netherlands and Norway gender gaps are smaller, with around two male suicides for each female death.

Older people are more likely to take their own lives, but this pattern is not general across the OECD. Greece, Italy, Portugal and Korea are examples of countries where older people take their own lives more often than young people (CO4.3). The largest increasing age gradient is found in Korea. Korean suicide rates by age show a steep increase from the ages of 45-54. Furthermore, rates amongst the eldest group (75 years or more) are more than ten times higher than those of young people aged 15-24. The upward Korean suicide trend of recent years is partly explained by a strong rise in suicide by older people. By contrast, in a minority of OECD countries – for example New Zealand and Norway – young people are more likely to take their own lives than older people.

Differences in suicide rates between males and females usually rise with age. For example, on average across the OECD the age 15-19 male suicide rate is 2.7 times that of females of the same age, but that of males over 75 years of age is 5.3 times higher than for females (CO4.4). This pattern may reflect the higher social isolation, possibly following ending of a long term partnership by dissolution or death, of older males compared to older females.

Further reading

Sainsbury, P. and J.S. Jenkins (1982), "The Accuracy of Officially Reported Suicide Statistics for Purposes of Epidemiological Research", *Journal of Epidemiology and Community Health*, Vol. 36, pp. 43-48.

Figure note

Figures CO4.1 to CO4.4: 2004 for Canada, Germany, Netherlands and Sweden; 2003 for Australia, Italy and Portugal; 2001 for Denmark; 1997 for Belgium.

CO4.1. Falling suicide rates in most OECD countries

Suicides per 100 000 persons by age group, 2005

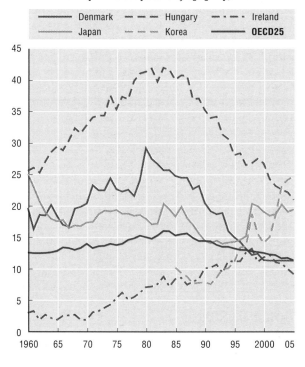

CO4.2. Higher suicides among men than women

Suicides per 100 000 persons across countries and gender, 2005

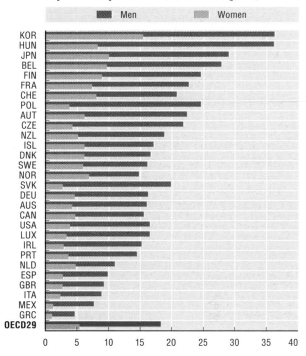

CO4.3. Suicide by age patterns vary by country

Suicides per 100 000 persons by age group, 2005

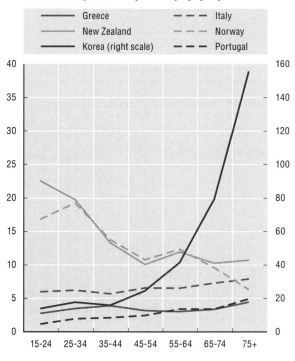

CO4.4. Gender difference in suicide higher amongst the elderly

Ratio of male to female suicide rates by selected age group, 2005

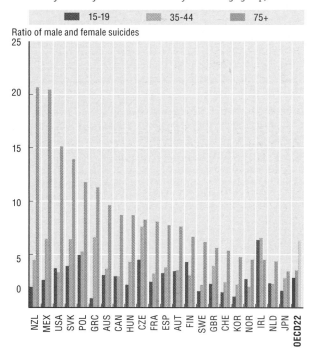

Source: Suicides from WHO Mortality database (*www.who.int/healthinfo/morttables/en/index.html*).

StatLink ⟲⟲ http://dx.doi.org/10.1787/550724182187

Definition and measurement

Bullying includes hitting and teasing, as well as more passive forms such as exclusion from conversations and play. Bullying does not include fighting between equally strong children. The broad definition of bullying does not show which forms are most prevalent in which country, or the duration and intensity of bullying.

Data are drawn from school-based samples from the *Health Behaviour in School-aged Children Survey* for the years 2005-06. Bullying estimates are calculated using reported rates of bullying and being bullied weighted by sample numbers for 11-, 13- and 15-year-old boys and girls. The proportions of first-generation migrant students at age 15 are based on self-reported statistics of country of birth published as part of the OECD PISA 2006 results.

Being a bully or being bullied is not uncommon. Around one in ten OECD children is a recent bullying victim, and the ratio of bullies is similar. Figure CO5.1 shows that children are most likely to have experienced bullying in Turkey and Greece. Bullying is least common in Sweden and Spain. Greece and Austria have the most bullies, whereas Sweden, the Czech Republic and Iceland have the fewest.

Perpetrators and victims of bullying are more likely to be boys than girls. Only in Hungary and Greece are girls victims of bullying more often than, or equal to, boys. There are no countries with more female than male perpetrators.

Bullies slightly outnumber the bullied, suggesting that bullying is performed in groups. Observational research on bullying suggests that between 80 and 90% of episodes are attended by other children: three-quarters of whom reinforce the bullying beha-viour, or at least do not challenge it (Atlas *et al.*, 1998; and Hawkins *et al.*, 2001). For boys there is no clear rela-tionship across countries between the number of bul-lies and the number of victims. For girls it is a little clearer, with more girls being bullied than bullying, which may reflect cases of boys bullying girls or girls more reluctant to admit or acknowledge bullying.

Bullying generally increases as children get older (CO5.2). As children get older, and spend more time in school, patterns of bullying change. For boys the increase with age is more marked, particularly in Greece, Luxembourg, Austria and Germany. Only Turkey reports a drop in bullying for both boys and girls with age, though absolute levels in that country remain comparatively high.

There is more bullying at age 15 in countries where there are more 15-year-old migrant students (CO5.3) When children bully in groups, or where bullying is part of normal group behaviour, research suggests that friendships are made and maintained in part to show a distinction from other groups, or individuals (Duffy and Nesdale, 2008). The cross-national evidence provides some support for this hypothesis.

Further reading

Atlas, R. *et al.* (1998), "Observations of Bullying in the Classroom", *Journal of Educational Research*, Vol. 92, pp. 86-99.

Currie, C. et al. (2008), *Inequalities in Young People's Health: HBSC International Report,* WHO Regional Office for Europe, Copenhagen, Denmark.

Duffy, A. and D. Nesdale (2008), "Peer Groups, Social Identity and Children's Bullying Behaviour", *Social Development,* pp. 1-19.

Hawkins, L. *et al.* (2001), "Naturalistic Observations of Peer Interventions in Bullying", *Social Development*, Vol. 10, No. 4, pp. 512-527.

OECD (2008), *PISA 2006 Database*, OECD, Paris.

Table note

Table CO5.2: Australia, New Zealand, Japan, Korea, Norway, Ireland, the United States, Turkey and Mexico are missing. Data for Belgium is Flemish Belgium only. Data for the United Kingdom does not include Northern Ireland.

CO5.1. Boys are more often both victim and perpetrator of bullying

Victimisation and perpetration by gender, countries ranked by total average perpetration percentage

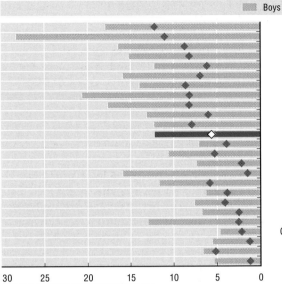
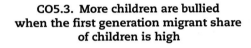
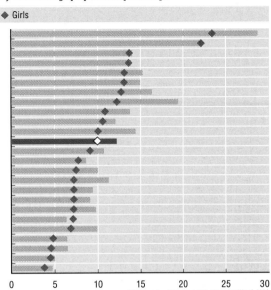

Children who report bullying others (%)

Children who report being bullied (%)

CO5.2. Bullying is more common amongst older children

	Girls			Boys		
	11 years	13 years	15 years	11 years	13 years	15 years
Austria	5	11	11	11	26	26
Belgium	6	6	7	12	11	14
Canada	6	8	5	10	13	13
Czech Republic	2	3	2	3	6	5
Denmark	2	6	5	7	11	15
Finland	2	4	2	5	6	8
France	6	11	8	13	15	18
Germany	5	7	9	9	17	21
Greece	8	13	12	16	28	38
Hungary	2	4	2	3	7	10
Iceland	2	1	1	5	6	6
Ireland	2	3	2	6	7	9
Italy	7	6	5	13	12	14
Luxembourg	7	9	10	8	16	24
Netherlands	3	4	5	11	12	12
Norway	1	1	3	8	5	10
Poland	4	6	6	15	14	18
Portugal	8	9	8	14	15	13
Spain	4	6	6	5	8	7
Sweden	1	1	2	3	4	9
Switzerland	5	10	10	13	19	21
Turkey	16	13	7	21	19	13
Great Britain	2	5	6	4	8	10
United States	8	9	7	11	14	14
OECD24	**5**	**6**	**6**	**9**	**12**	**14**

CO5.3. More children are bullied when the first generation migrant share of children is high

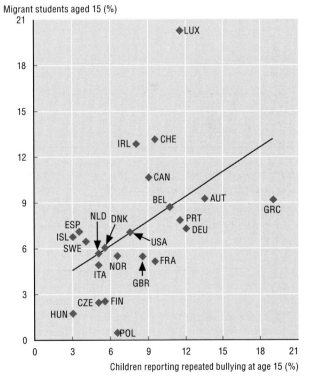

Migrant students aged 15 (%)

Children reporting repeated bullying at age 15 (%)

Source: *Inequalities in Young People's Health: HBSC International Report* (Currie *et al*, 2008). OECD PISA (2008).

StatLink 🖳 http://dx.doi.org/10.1787/550735513761

Definition and measurement

Risky behaviour refers to actions undertaken by children that are normally considered adult behaviours, and which can negatively affect their lives. Levels of risky behaviour in each country show the extent to which children are receiving suitable guardianship or information regarding age appropriate activities. Risky behaviour indicators include rates and trends of self-reported excessive drinking and regular smoking in early adolescence. As well, risky behaviour includes self-reported rates of early sexual experiences, and non-use of condoms to protect against unwanted pregnancy and sexually transmitted diseases.

Data for risky behaviour indicators are taken from the *Health Behaviour in School-aged Children Survey 2005/06* (HBSC). Twenty-five OECD countries are included in the survey. However some countries choose not to ask children questions about drinking, smoking or sex. Country estimates are calculated using reported rates and sample numbers for 15-year-old boys and girls. For rates of drunkenness results for the 13-year-old cohort are also included.

Considerable numbers of girls and boys smoke and get drunk. Girls smoke more than boys, but boys are more likely to get drunk. In 2005-06 smoking was especially popular amongst Austrian girls and Finnish boys, and least popular amongst boys in the United States and Canada. Rates by sex by country ranged from 7% to 30%. Drunkenness did not vary quite so starkly. Getting drunk repeatedly was most prevalent amongst boys in the United Kingdom and Denmark and least common amongst Italian and Swiss girls (CO6.1).

Alcohol and cigarette consumption amongst 15-year-olds is falling from a high recorded in the late 1990s. Country convergence in risk behaviours is also evident as overall rates fall amongst girls for smoking, and drunkenness for both sexes. With the exception of Greece all countries report declining rates in youth smoking for both boys and girls. Levels of smoking for both sexes are at their lowest for a decade, with less than one in five children of either sex smoking regularly. There have been large reductions in drunkenness in Denmark, Finland and the United Kingdom, where youth historically have high levels of alcohol abuse. At the national level increasing rates of drunkenness among boys are rare. Five countries – Austria, France, Italy, Poland and Spain – report increases. Of these only Austria and Poland were high to start with. Perhaps less surprisingly drunkenness amongst girls is also falling. However an increase for drunkenness amongst girls is seen in Hungary which is not matched by a similar increase for boys.

One quarter of 15-year-old boys and girls report early sexual experiences (CO6.2). There is not a great deal of variation between countries, with all but two reporting rates within 10% either side of the average. There is a fairly robust geographical divide in early sexual experiences between the sexes. Early sexual experiences are more prevalent for boys in Mediterranean countries, and more prevalent for girls in northern European countries.

One quarter of 15-year-old boys and girls who had an early sexual experience did not use a condom in their last sexual encounter. With only 16 OECD countries providing rates, data for condom use is limited. Nine OECD countries participating in the HBSC survey chose not to ask for this information from their 15-year-old children. Around three in four children report using appropriate protection during their last sexual intercourse, ranging from a low of 70% to a high of around 90%. In almost all countries girls use condoms less than boys.

Further reading

Currie, C. et al. (2008), *Inequalities in Young People's Health: HBSC International Report*, WHO Regional Office for Europe, Copenhagen, Denmark.

Figure and table notes

Table CO6.1: UK figures are for England only. Belgium figures are a simple average of Flemish and French-speaking figures for each wave except 1997-98 when French-speaking Belgium did not participate. The OECD average is calculated using reported figures for each wave. Cigarette smoking is for smoking at least one cigarette during the past week and is for 15-year-olds only. Drunkenness shows the proportion of children aged 13 and 15 who report ever having been drunk 2-3 times or more (sample weights are used to calculate averages between age cohorts). The actual question was "Have you ever had so much alcohol that you were really drunk?". Australia, New Zealand, Mexico, Japan, Korea and Mexico are missing.

Figure CO6.2: Australia, New Zealand, Japan, Korea, Norway, Ireland, the United States, Turkey and Mexico are missing. Iceland, Luxembourg, Italy and the Czech Republic do not ask children about condom use. Data for Belgium is Flemish Belgium only. Data for the United Kingdom does not include Northern Ireland. The sexual intercourse question asked children aged 15 whether they had ever had sexual intercourse. The condom question was "The last time you had sex did you or your partner use a condom?".

CO6.1. Cigarette smoking and drunkenness amongst teen-aged children is falling from highs in the 1990s

Rates of cigarette smoking and repeated drunkenness of teen-aged boys and girls, percentages, 1993-94 to 2005-06

| | Regular cigarette smoking (15 year olds only) | | | | | | | | Repeated drunkenness (13 and 15 year olds) | | | | | | | |
| | Boys | | | | Girls | | | | Boys | | | | Girls | | | |
	1993-94	1997-98	2001-02	2005-06	1993-94	1997-98	2001-02	2005-06	1993-94	1997-98	2001-02	2005-06	1993-94	1997-98	2001-02	2005-06
Austria	29	30	26	24	31	36	37	30	31	30	22	25	20	21	19	21
Belgium	28	28	22	16	20	28	24	17	20	22	22	21	12	14	15	14
Canada	21	21	16	7	28	26	14	10	27	29	28	24	25	28	26	25
Czech Republic	16	22	29	20	12	18	31	23	24	25	25	25	13	14	18	20
Denmark	14	20	17	15	24	28	21	15	45	46	45	34	43	40	39	29
Finland	30	25	28	23	26	29	32	21	35	34	36	29	32	37	37	27
France	23	28	26	17	25	31	27	21	15	18	13	16	8	12	9	12
Germany	21	28	32	17	29	33	34	22	20	23	28	19	16	19	22	17
Greece	..	18	14	17	..	19	14	16	..	17	17	15	..	13	11	11
Hungary	25	36	28	22	19	28	26	21	22	22	29	26	12	11	16	20
Iceland	..	..	..	14	..	..	..	13	..	..	..	14	..	..	..	13
Ireland		25	20	19	..	25	21	20	..	29	21	23	..	19	19	19
Italy	..	..	22	20	..	..	25	20	..	..	14	15	..	..	10	10
Luxembourg	..	..	..	17	..	..	..	21	..	..	..	16	..	..	..	12
Netherlands	..	..	23	16	..	..	24	21	..	..	22	17	..	..	14	13
Norway	20	23	20	9	21	28	27	12	17	22	22	14	15	23	23	17
Poland	23	27	26	19	13	20	17	14	24	27	27	30	12	14	16	19
Portugal	..	19	18	9	..	14	26	12	..	22	20	17	..	10	14	13
Slovakia	19	28	..	18	5	18	..	15	32	32	..	27	13	19	..	21
Spain	20	..	24	14	27	..	32	20	14	..	25	17	11	22	23	16
Sweden	15	18	11	8	19	24	19	9	14	23	23	17	7	9	15	11
Switzerland	17	25	25	15	18	25	24	18	13	15	23	17	..	36	40	33
United Kingdom	..	25	21	13	..	33	28	18	..	37	42	32	..	36	40	33
United States	..	20	18	7	..	21	12	9	..	23	18	12	..	20	14	12

—— OECD average

- - - Standard deviation

(Four line charts: vertical axis 0–40; horizontal axis 1993-94, 1997-98, 2001-02, 2005-06)

CO6.2. One in four 15-year-olds have had sex, often without adequate protection

Sexual activity and condom use amongst 15-year-olds, in percentage

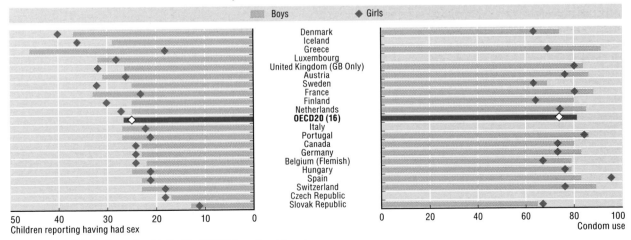

Boys ▮ Girls ◆

Denmark
Iceland
Greece
Luxembourg
United Kingdom (GB Only)
Austria
Sweden
France
Finland
Netherlands
OECD20 (16)
Italy
Portugal
Canada
Germany
Belgium (Flemish)
Hungary
Spain
Switzerland
Czech Republic
Slovak Republic

(Left axis) Children reporting having had sex — 50 40 30 20 10 0

(Right axis) Condom use — 0 20 40 60 80 100

Source: *Inequalities in Young People's Health: HBSC International Report* (Currie et al., 2008).

StatLink ᔐᕐ http://dx.doi.org/10.1787/550737414418

OECD PUBLISHING, 2, rue André-Pascal, 75775 PARIS CEDEX 16
PRINTED IN FRANCE
(81 2009 01 1 P) ISBN 978-92-64-04938-3 – No. 56663 2009